MODERN ARCHITECTURE
IN THAILAND

01

PAGE●ONE

Modern Architecture in Thailand 01
Copyright © 2010 Li-Zenn Publishing Limited

First published in 2010 by
Li-Zenn Publishing Limited
81 Sukhumvit 26 Bangkok 10110
T: 66(0) 2259-2096
F: 66(0) 2667-2017
www.li-zenn.com

Published in Asia in 2010 by
Page One Publishing Pte Ltd
20 Kaki Bukit View Kaki Bukit Techpark II
Singapore 415956
Tel: (65) 6742-2088
Fax: (65) 6744-2088
enquiries@pageonegroup.com
www.pageonegroup.com

Li-Zenn

Text, design and layout copyright © 2010
Li-Zenn Publishing Limited
81 Sukhumvit 26 Bangkok 10110 Thailand
T: +66 (0) 2259 2096, F: +66 (0) 2661 2017
li-zenn@li-zenn.com, www.li-zenn.com

ISBN 978-981-245-968-8

Printed in China

MODERN ARCHITECTURE
IN THAILAND

01

Contents

Transportation

012 Suvarnabhumi International Airport
020 Suvarnabhumi Airport Rail Link and City Air Terminal
030 Samui International Airport

Mixed Use

036 King Power Complex
046 Interchange 21

Commercial

050 Century the Movie Plaza
052 Suvarnabhumi Honda Automobile
056 Central Plaza Khon Kaen
060 The 49 Terrace
064 Siam Paragon Shopping Center
068 Uawithya Showroom
072 Workpoint Studio Village
080 Amari Residences Hua Hin Street Side Restaurant
084 Practika Factory
088 Maze
090 Harbormall
092 Esplanade & Ratchadalai Theater
096 K Village
098 Mini Showroom
102 Honda Big Wing

Office

108 Chai Tour Office
112 Architect Council of Thailand
116 Energy Complex
122 Royal Archive
130 Crew Training Center (Renovation)
134 Operation Center
138 Thailand Elite Headquarters
142 Community Organization Development Institute (CODI)
148 Stepwise Group Headquarter
150 Osotspa Building 3
154 Osotspa Canteen
158 Sun One
166 Sala @ Sathorn
170 Phuket Gateway
174 PM Center Office Building
180 Bank of Thailand Headquarter
186 The Office Plus
190 Q. House Lumpini Park

Culture

196 SCG Experience
202 The Oriental Fine Art
206 Exhibition Gallery, Chulalongkorn University
210 The First Royal Factory at Fang the Museum
214 Pleanwan
220 Prince of Songkhlar University International Convention Center
226 Henry B Thompson Building

Education

232 BU Landmark Complex
238 Arsom Silp Institute of the Arts and Development
246 Dr. Arthit Urairat Building, Rangsit University
250 College of Medicine and Public Health
254 Bangkok University Admission and Information Center
258 Bangkok University International College and Art Gallery
264 College of Music, Mahidol University

In this day and age many countries around the world especially those in Asia have open-door policies in areas of free trade and services. Furthermore, this is an era when communication is swift allowing for boundless communication of knowledge leading to many areas of economic expansion and urban development. Large scale construction can be seen continually over many decades in major cities all over the Asian region. As a result we see the converging of architects and engineers from all areas taking part in creating beautiful and outstanding designs in important cities. Consequently, we can see fierce professional competition from architects, engineers and interior designers, Thai architects and interior designers took on the impact of this changing trend. Work strategies needed to be adjusted in order to keep pace with this major change. It is important for architects and interior designers in this region to come together in order to show the world their potential and capabilities. There must be opportunities for exchange of views which supports the progress of professional development. The process of disseminating useful information which is beneficial to those in the profession and as well as to the public is a way of ensuring that there is steady and strong development for this profession. This will be evident to the world and we also need to create an understanding on the soul and essence of arts and cultures and the architectural work being constructed in this region.

The modern Thai architecture evolved continuously through many eras over a period of hundreds of years. The contributing factor towards this development was through the soul and imagination of folk artisans and local artists, in combination with western arts and cultures brought on by European architects and engineers. They have worked within the walls of palaces from the Ayutthaya era (A.D. 1350-1767) to the Thonburi (A.D. 1767-1782) and Rattanakosin (A.D. 1782-present) eras. Thai architects and artisans have always been very articulate, meticulous and creative and these values have been brought down to this current era. Today, we can see Thai architects and interior designers creating a lot of modern architecture, its beauty and uniqueness are evident to visitors. There are many more architectural works yet to be discovered, many people did not have the opportunity to see these works which are spread out around the country, some are on the mountains, in the forests while some are privately owned and outsiders are not allowed to see them.

It has always been my aspiration to compile and showcase to the world Thailand's architecture and interior design I would like to publicize the works of Thailand's architects and interior designers. In Thailand there have never been attempts to publish such books for the international market, whatever the reasons may be, the question lingers continually in my mind. I had the opportunity to raise this issue with several friends who are architects and interior designers expressing my desire to compile modern architecture and interior design works in Thailand and publish them in a book which is of international standard, a book which is valuable and beautifully presented enough to be placed alongside other publications of its kind on the bookstand in other countries. The idea was quickly endorsed by all my architect friends, everyone agreed to give their support on the matter.

It is widely known that development in modern architecture and interior design in Thailand evolved over a period of over 100 years, we can see modern architecture and interior design being produced all over the country, the works are the results of designs by both Thai and foreign architects. This is especially within the last 5-10 years when we can see many interesting modern buildings being designed, designs which are worth being showcased to the world. These works show great clarity and profoundness in design, many buildings are majestic in appearance revealing strong identity in their specific city location, and they are a pride to the country and those who see them.

When I first kick-started the compilation process, I received positive responses from large numbers of my architect friends who forwarded pictures of over 300 different projects for selection. This response greatly encouraged me. My ambition to see this book become a reality was increasingly eminent before me. Finally, my team and I decided upon designs from over 160 different projects which consisted of 110 architecture projects and 60 interior design projects.

I wish to express my appreciation to all the architects and interior designers who showed their consistent support to me and in particular their encouragement when I first initiated the idea to publish this book right up to the finalization which consisted of a large number of selected projects. As a result, our team decided to group the projects into three books to be called 'modern Architecture in Thailand 001', 'modern Architecture in Thailand 002' and 'modern Interior in Thailand 003', all consisting of the appropriate number of pages, allowing for essential details to be featured in the contents.

I hope that three books can truly represent Thailand's architects and interior designers who greatly contributed to the design works in Thailand. It is hoped that the books can portray to the world the capability and determination of Thai architects and interior designers.

I would like to thank all architects and interior designers who supported this publication by forwarding their works, my thanks also to the publishing team at 'Li-Zenn Publishing Limited' for turning my ambition into reality and lastly my appreciation to those who supported us financially towards the publication and completion of this book.

Nithi Sthapitanonda
Editor

Suvarnabhumi International Airport

Location :
Bang Phli, Samut Prakan

Client :
Airport of Thailand

Area :
563,000 sq.m.

Year :
1994-2006

The primary objective is to build a 21st century airport for the people of Thailand. It should be clearly unique to Bangkok, inspiring and symbolic of Thailand in the next century.

A large roof trellis structure placed over the complex of functionally separate buildings unifies the site and provides an overriding consistent architectural image.

The buildings under the trellis take their architectural form from the function that they serve. At the intersection of the tubular concourses are cylindrical rotundas sky –lit roof structures. The concourses are tubular in shape deriving their architecture from their structure, a three hinged cable stayed arch.

The fundamental design concept for the terminal building and the concourses makes optimal use of the massing orientation and configuration to provide environmental comfort with minimal energy consumption. This is achieved by maximizing the impact of various architectural elements to create bright and airy spaces, while minimizing the use of artificial illumination and mechanical cooling systems.

Given the locale and its position to the equator, the linear orientation of the building with predominant north and south facades allows for the extensive use of natural versus artificial illumination, while screening out the thermal impact of the sun through use of fixed architectural elements. The roof design allows huge amounts of daylight to penetrate the space, creating a bright environment that minimizes the need for artificial illumination.

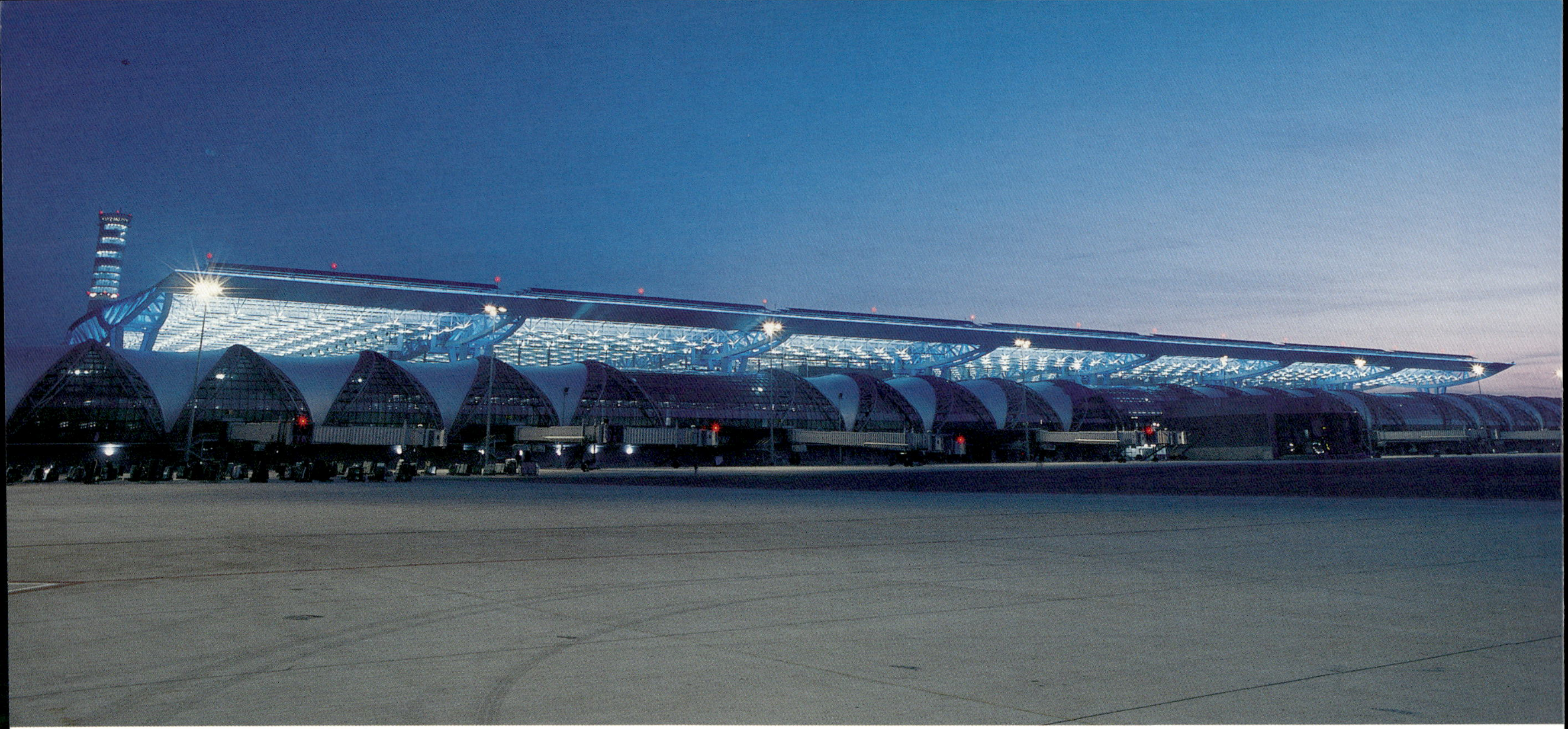

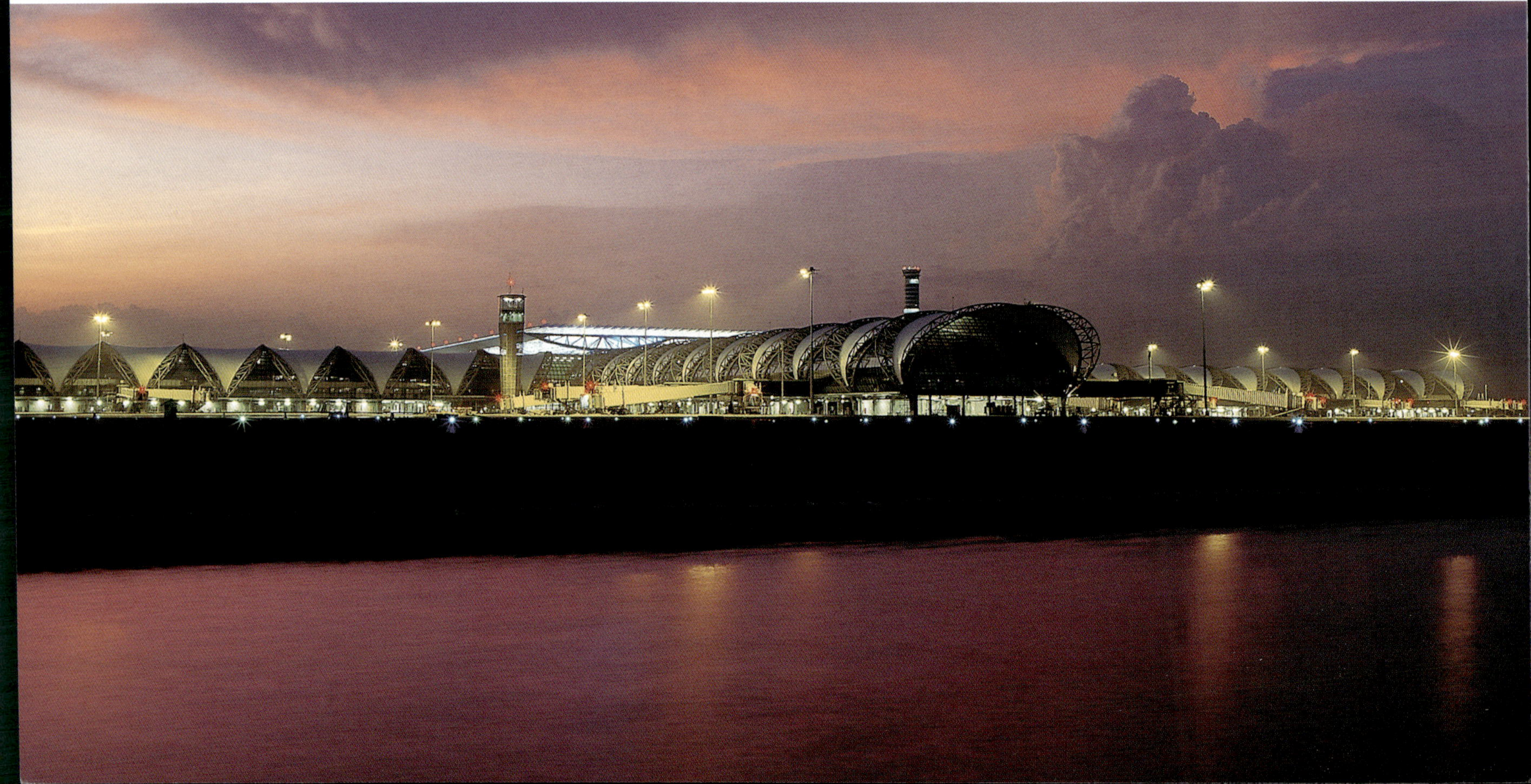

Adapting traditional architectural forms and recognizing high technology aspects of air travel.

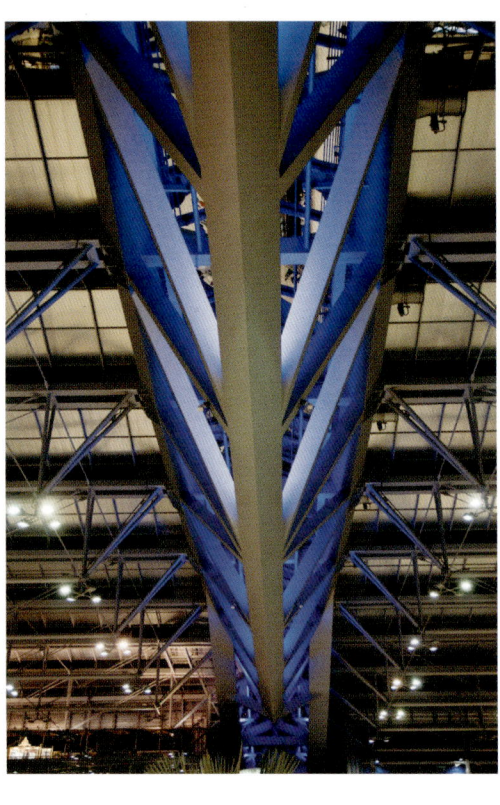

Outdoor spaces between the building are shaded by roof trellis.

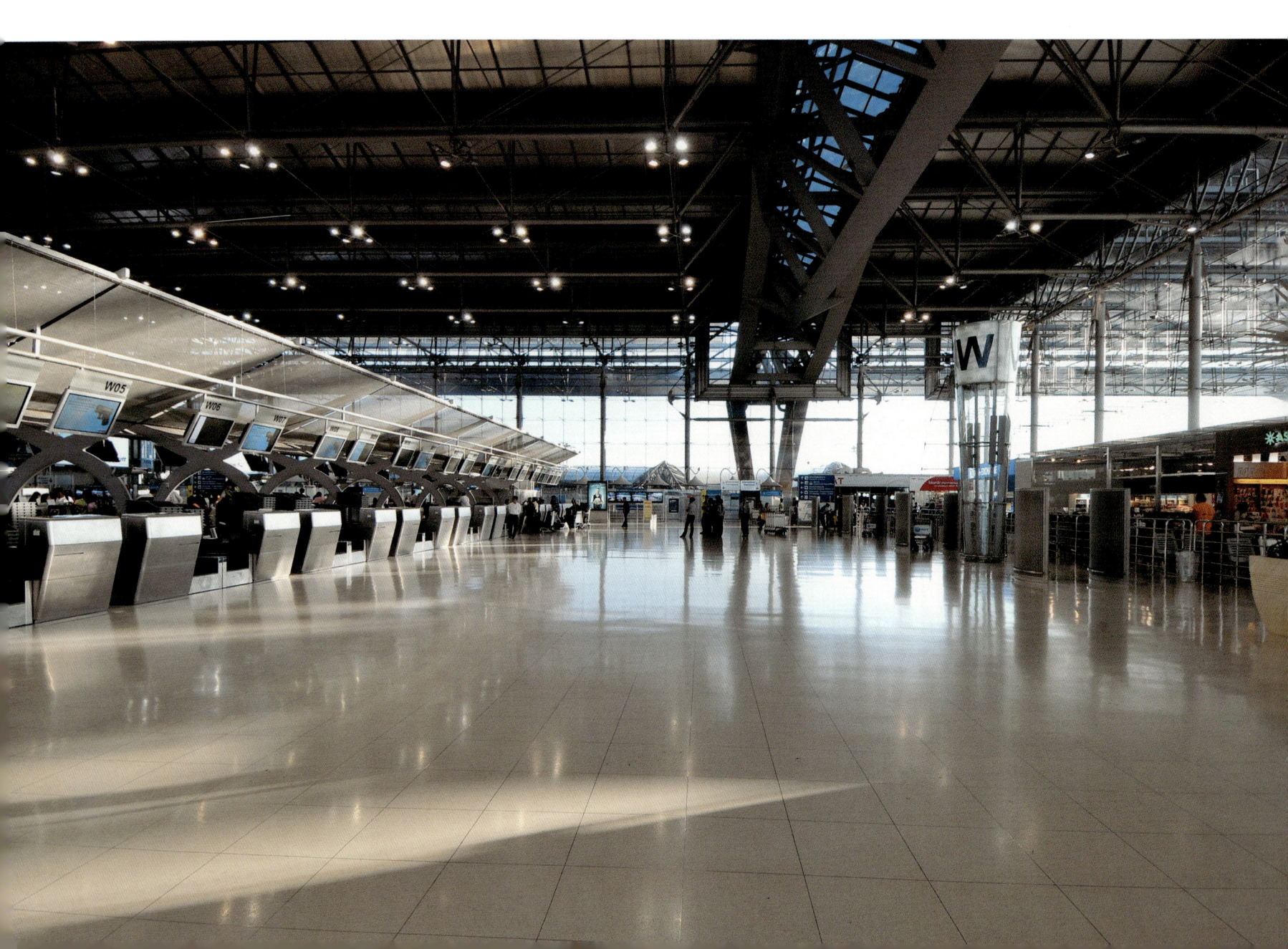

Cylindrical rotundas and tubular concourses with
the skylit roof structure.

002

Suvarnabhumi Airport Rail Link and City Air Terminal
Design Concept

Location :
East Line Railway, Bangkok

Client :
The State Railway of Thailand

Year :
2004-2009

The Suvarnabhumi Airport Rail Link and City Air Terminal (SARL) project supports and maximizes the new airport's service level. The SARL project is Thailand's first stand-alone, high-speed electric double-tracked railway system. The railway line is built parallel to the existing east line linking the inner city with the Suvarnabhumi Airport (SA). There are 8 stations, the Bangkok City Air Terminal (BCAT) and the maintenance depot and workshops. The main train operations and supporting services are comprised of three elements:

SA Express (Suvarnabhumi Airport Express): The rapid non-stop transit train system.

SA City Line (Suvarnabhumi Airport City Line): The commuter train.

Bangkok City Air Terminal (BCAT): Air passengers receive in-town ticketing and baggage check-in before traveling to the airport.

The main architectural features were designed to relate to the airport. The repeated use of triangular and curved shapes and the natural material color scheme were integrated into the edifice Building sustainability heavily influenced the structural plans. Planners carefully selected materials and MEP systems based on environmental friendliness and low energy consumption. Natural lighting and ventilation were included in the project where possible.

The design concept and use of materials and color was intended to create a modern public transportation building with unique architecture that is surrounded by elevated roads and high rise buildings.

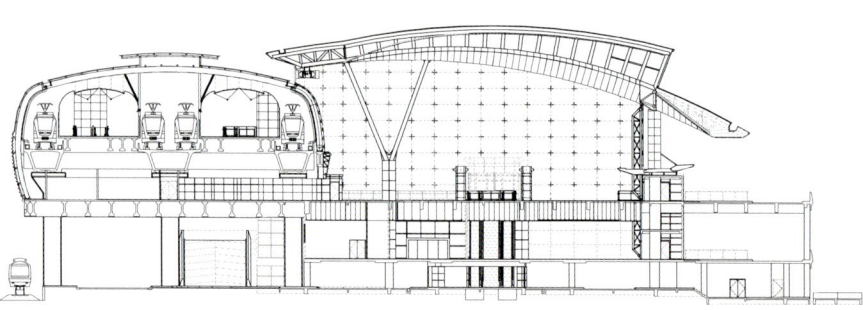

Clerestories stories above the terminal's roof.

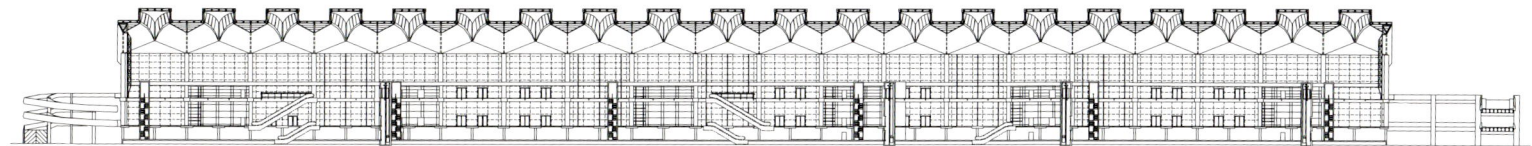

Bangkok City Air Terminal 86,500 sq.m.

Main canopy over drop-off curb on departure level.

1   2

1. Passenger arrival hall
2. Passenger check-in area on departure level.

City Line Passenger Hall inside Bangkok City Air Terminal

Tension Truss supported structural glass facade
at North side.

Hua Mak station

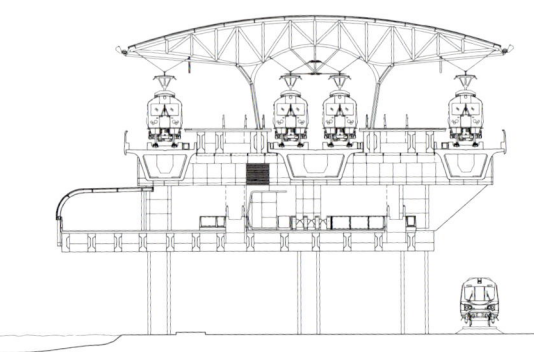

Ramkhamhaeng station

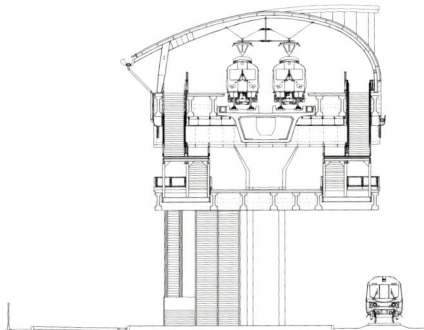
Ramkhamhaeng station

Ban Thap Chang station

Platform level at intermediate station showing sound treatment using perforated metal ceiling.

Platform level of intermediate station.

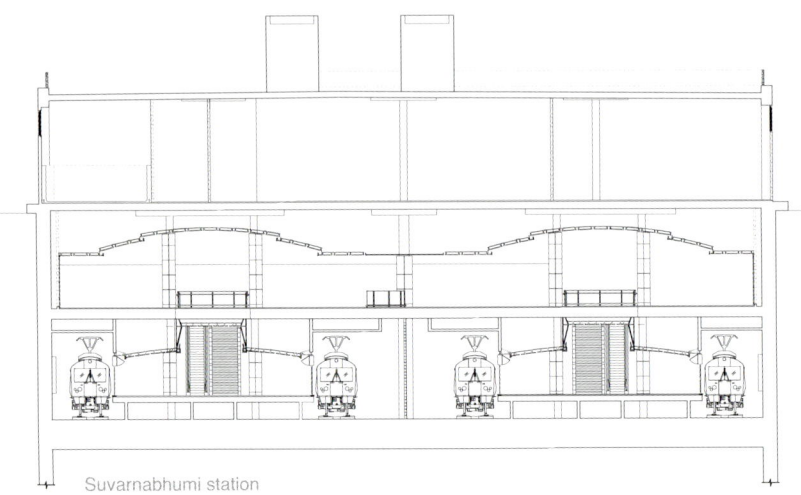

Suvarnabhumi station

City line concourse level at Suvarnabhumi station

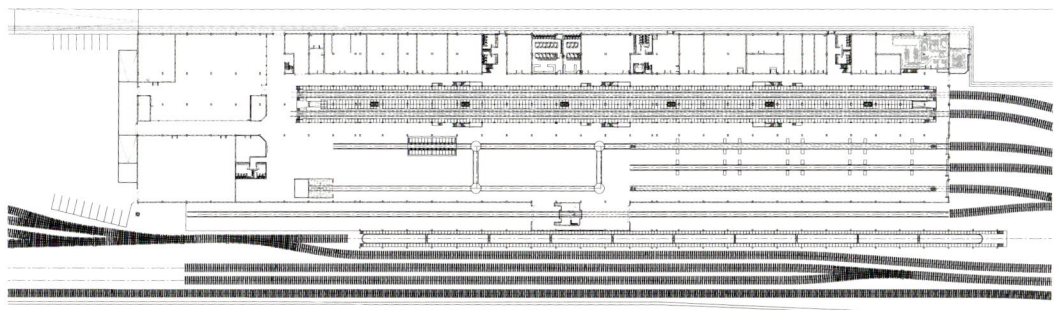

Depot & workshop building main workshop composed of operation control centre and rolling stocks maintenance facilities.

Depot and work shop

003

Location : Samui Island, Surajthani

Client : Bangkok Airways

Area : 29,027 sq.m.

Year : 2007

Samui International Airport   Habita

The island is fully covered with natural architecture, mostly coconut farms, and by coconut tree trunks, leaves, and branches. This natural architecture inspires the interior spaces below. Both visitors and locals experience the same natural patterns of dense, high coconut tree trunks which look like column structures. These trunks support the coconut leaf roof which splits out from the trees to provide the natural shelter for sunlight and rain protection. The natural light gets through the leaves to create complex pattern shadow that changes according to the sea breeze direction. These natural inspirations have influenced the main design concept to express the natural architectural symbolism throughout the airport building.

The interior roof structure is designed to imitate coconut branches and leaves, with the shade from weaving timber lath filtering natural light through the sky light. The open-air building's center conveys the feeling of sitting under the canopy of a coconut farm; a relaxing breeze blowing softly throughout.

With the energy saving concept above, each function must be separated into small sections for enough light and air flow, and surrounded by a pond for evaporated cooling. The pond is also used for the Departure Lounge and creates the 'Departure Island'. It also provides an outdoor space and garden within the departure area. The design of Departure Lounge is different from other airports which surprises passengers.

The natural light skylight provides enough light into the building to preclude using electric light during the day. The two-tiered roof is designed to provide an air ventilation gap and to avoid heat collection below, which could cause passenger discomfort.

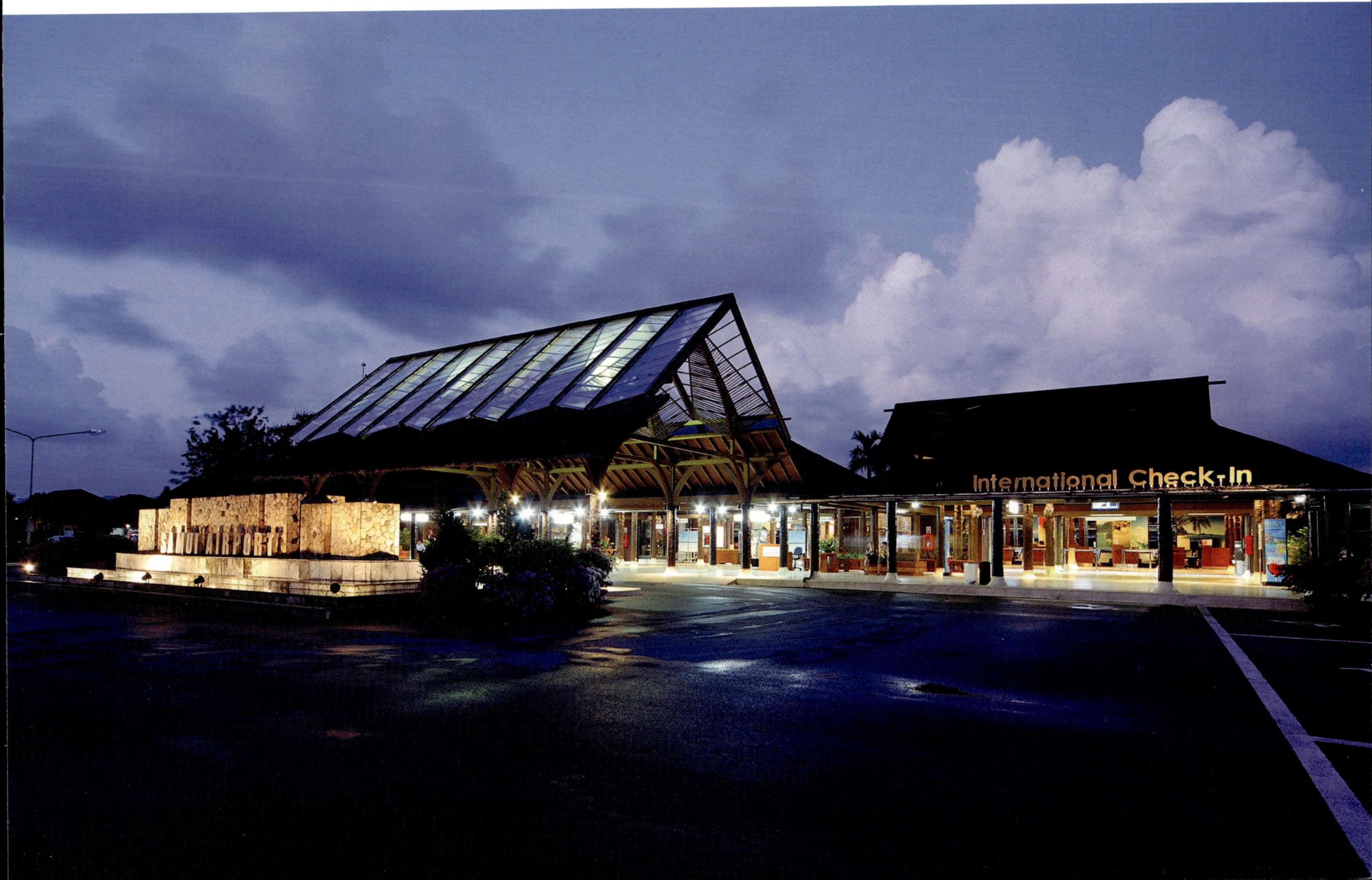

004

King Power Complex   Architects 49

Location :
Rang Nam Road, Bangkok

Client :
King Power International Group

Area :
145,000 sq.m.

Year :
2004-2007

The King Power Complex, located on 5.28 hectares in the heart of Bangkok, features a 12,000 SQ.M. Duty-Free Mall, the King Power headquarters, a 570-seat theater and dining facility and a 388-room 4-star hotel.

The Complex: King Power Complex is the destination of choice for travelers because of its visionary design and functionality. The development is a cultural phenomenon that provides a revolutionary shopping experience while architecturally celebrating Thailand's rich heritage.

Crown Atrium: Serving as the center of pedestrian circulation, the Crown Atrium is designed to express the connection between Thailand's past and present. Visually inspired by the pattern of ancient Thai gold ware, the Crown Atrium is engineered with advanced technology to search for the equilibrium between the construction method, the energy, the light, temperature and construction cost. With its scale and context condition, the Crown Atrium has already become a symbol of the area and might well become another Bangkok icon.

Headquarters: From the main entrance to the lobby, eight full floors of open area connect to the office center atrium. A glazed elevator and exposed staircases stretch to the top. This tremendous space generates an exciting working atmosphere which is humanized by streams of natural sun light and ventilation. The offices are elegantly designed with four meters floor to ceiling height creating the highest standard of working conditions.

Hotel: With 430 guest rooms, the King Power hotel occupies the twenty one-floor south wing tower. The inner courtyard is surrounded from the west and north by six floors of suite rooms. First level guest rooms are treated to the intimated touch of the waterscape. The King Power hotel is the result of mingling the simplicity of tropical oriental style with the modern lines and new construction material.

Office central atrium

Drop-off of King Power Headquaters

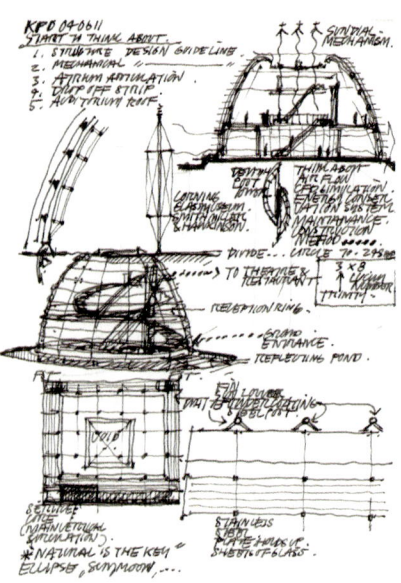

Inner crown atrium

Pullman Bangkok Hotel and Resort, a part of King Power Complex.

Inner courtyard surrounded by the six floors of suite rooms.

005

Interchange 21   Palmer & Turner (Thailand)

Location :
Sukhumvit 21 Road, Bangkok

Client :
B&G Park

Area :
103,398 sq.m.

Year :
2004-2008

The 30-storey tower and 2-level basement mixed-use complex is comprised of office and retail space with a direct connection to the MRTA subway and BTS sky train stations. The plan form of the building is generally rectangular in shape and parallel to the site boundary line, with the front podium portion angled diagonally toward the main junction in order to reflect the cityscape.

The curvilinear shape of the podium portion responds to the main frontage of the development and maximizes the valuable facade facing the junction. The office tower features column free office space with views overlooking the city and Benjakitti Park. The Low "E" glass facade and vertical fins add a rich context of sculptural definition to the building. These features, together with the horizontal sunshades, reduce heat gain and, thus, provide energy efficient savings to the building.

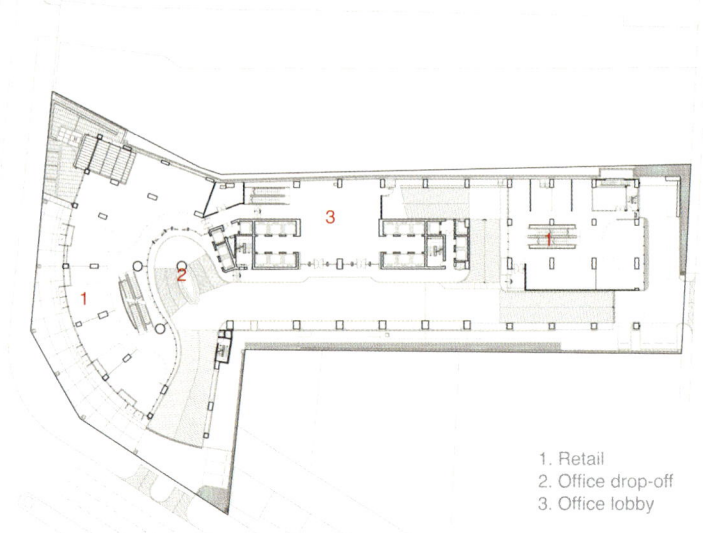

1. Retail
2. Office drop-off
3. Office lobby

DA VINCI
CODE
INTERCHANGE
INTERCHANGE
HOT
ICE

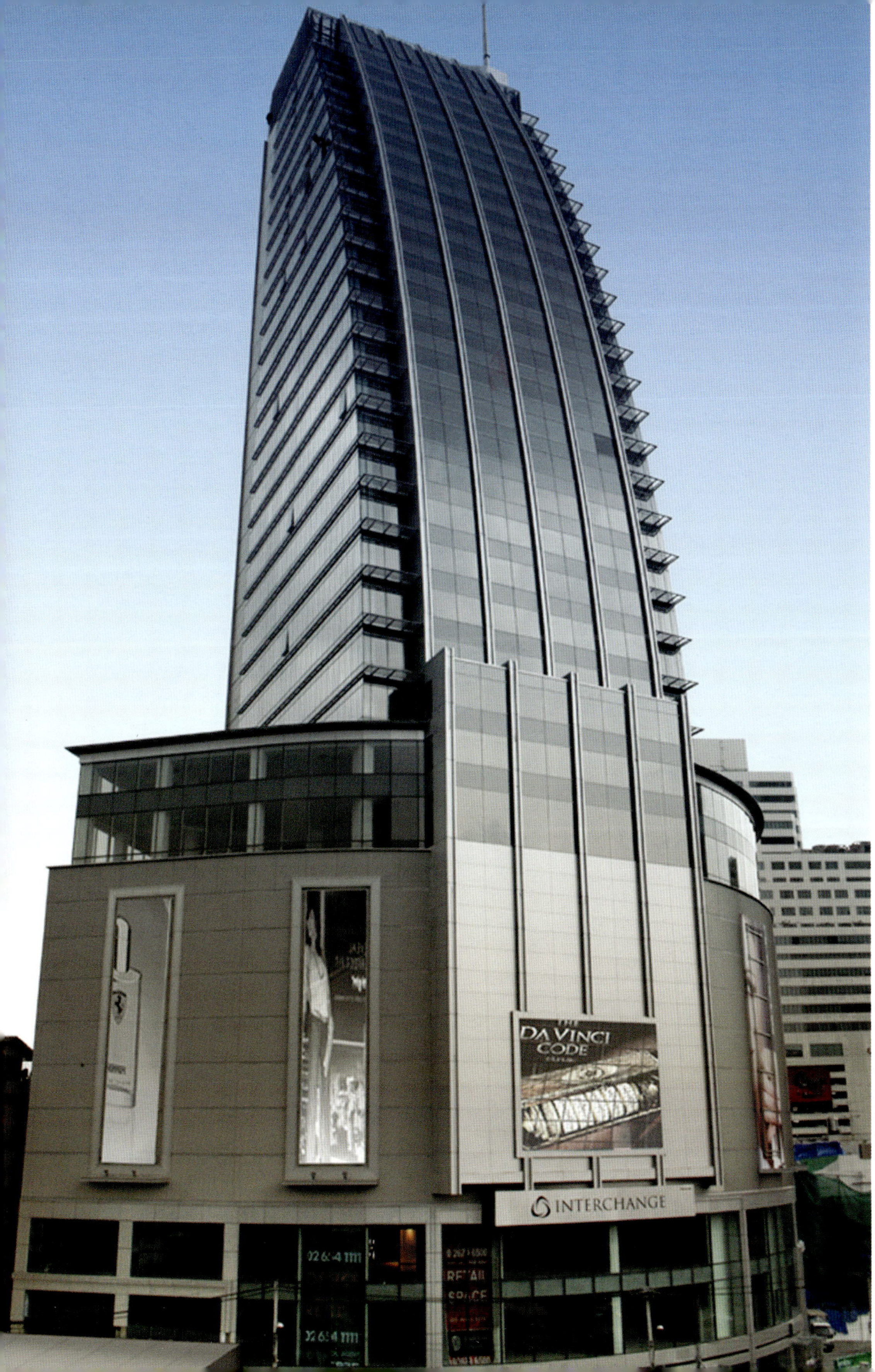

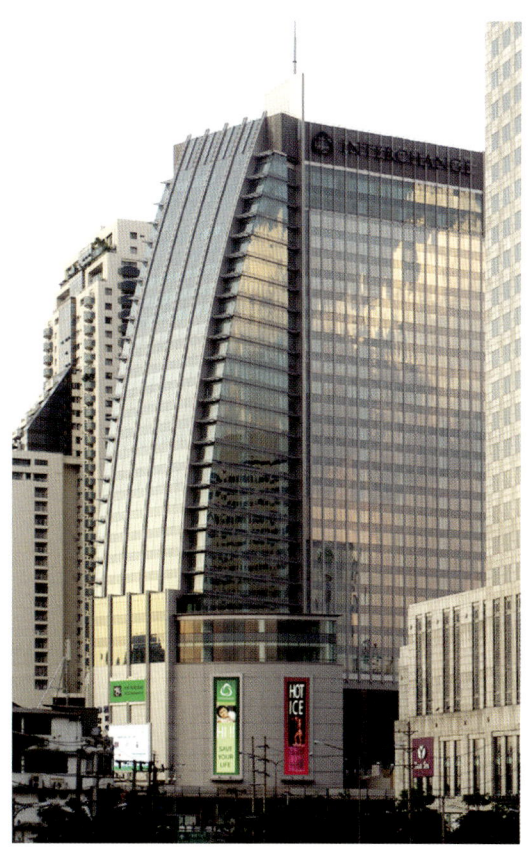

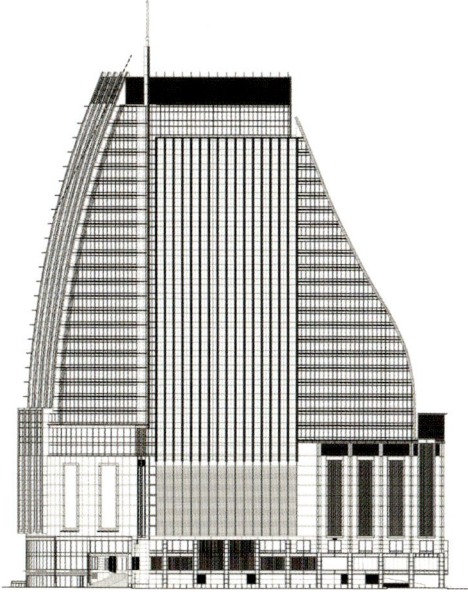

006

Century the Movie Plaza   Archer Architect

Location :
Phayathai Road, Phaya Thai, Bangkok

Client :   Ek Mahakit

Area :   50,000 sq.m.

Year :   2004-2005

Situated adjacent to the Skytrain station on Rang Num Road in Payathai, Bangkok, the 9-story, 50,000 square-meter Century Movie Plaza houses a retail shop, supermarket, exhibition area, movie theatre, fitness centre, education service, office and a 4-level, 400-car parking garage. Owned by Ek Mahakit Co., Ltd, the development projects the look of snapshot movements. The complex's design showcases aluminum composite to project a colorful, modern expression.

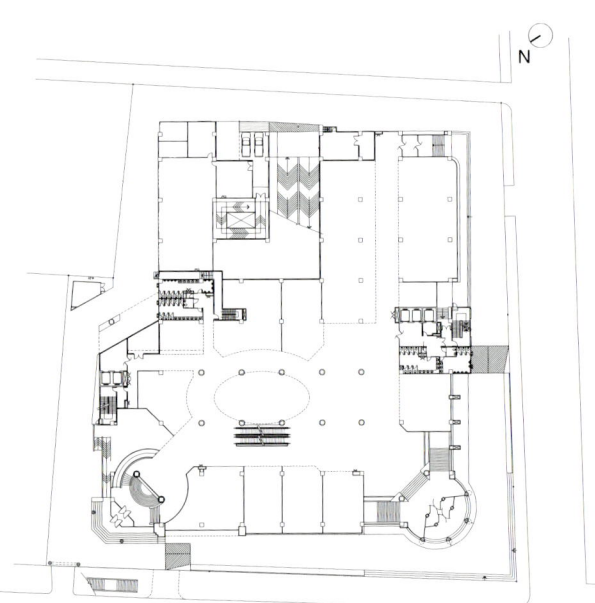

007

Suvarnabhumi Honda Automobile

Architects & Associates

Location : Bang Na-Trat Road, Samut Prakan

Client : Bang Phli Honda

Area : 7,250 sq.m.

Year : 2004-2006

Suvarnabhumi Honda Automobile is designed to establish a modern and futuristic landmark. The building frontage is approximately 90 meters. The architect breaks this lengthy span into 3 different functional parts and appearances.

The eastern test-drive parking and new car reception area has the lowest elevation (6 meters height) of all 3 sections, and is covered with a 16-meter wide metal roof. This part is kept simple and openly reflects its function.

Clear glass panels applied to the vertical front facade stretch to the top horizontal strip skylight, utilizing maximum daylight and making the middle area (showroom and customer service center) light and transparent. All inside background panels have white finishes; enhancing the displayed cars' visibility both outside and inside the showroom. A large front glass panel is located facing north to enjoy the efficient daylight. Double tier horizontal glass fins are incorporated on the front facade to distinguish the showroom glass box. The fins are frosted to add a more opaque quality and to create shadow. A series of supporting composite aluminum-clad steel ribs are placed systematically under the glass fins to enhance the feature.

The western section (drive-in reception area) has the highest elevation and is the end and focal point. Both concave and convex curves are integrated to a continuous plane of metal roof and wall coverings and the column-free space of drive-in reception area. The lower metal siding wall is cut out and fit with weaving, rhombus-shaped metal lines; creating more interesting mass/void and light/shadow features.

The structure is accented on a horizontal axis to reflect elegance and refinement. The showroom interior is lit at night to enhance curve of the ceiling and create a scattered light effect. The curved drive-in reception roof and wall area is bathed with ground up-light. The building has become one of the new landmarks on the Bangna-Trad highway by day and night.

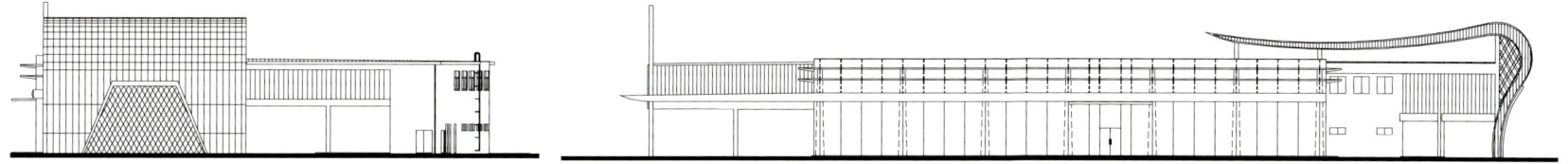

The glass box of the showroom is lit at night to distinguish from the overall building.

Mass / void and light / shadow displayed by rhombus shape weaving metal elements.

008

Location : Khon Kaen   **Client :** Central Pattana   **Area :** 72,500 sq.m.   **Year :** 2008-2009

Central Plaza Khon Kaen   Architects 49

Situated at the junction where gateway of Khon Kaen, the portal city of Thailand's northeastern business is located. 80 hectares compound resides opposite to the public park.

The area of 160,000 square meters is spitted into two structures functionally. The frontal is occupied with the retails. While, the rear serves mainly as a parking lot for 800 cars, with same certain functions on its roof, such as fitness club and convention center, leaving the lower parking lot to be conveniently connected to the commercial floors. The commercial floors are organized by so called the classic dumbbell system where the anchors function such as B2S, Super Sport, Power Buy and food court are placed at the end of circulation trajectory to attract visitors. The precise dimension from the workshop's conclusion delicately determined the floor to floor space. As for the first floor is at 5.2 meters while the upper floors are at 4.8 meters, with the average corridor width at 3 meters.

Inevitably, the project embraces the Isaan or Northeaster culture by implementing the articulation of intersection corner. Woven pattern of the handcraft project is distilled, enlarged and dematerialized by certain detail such as wire mesh and steel pattern. Wrapping around the anchor space where certain areas are exposed as outdoor space. The weaving pattern then unfolded to become the expressed elements to the other part of the project such as the entrance canopy or advertising banner.

Wire mesh and steel pattern folded as a weaving pattern.

A lighting design at a night scene.

centralplaZa

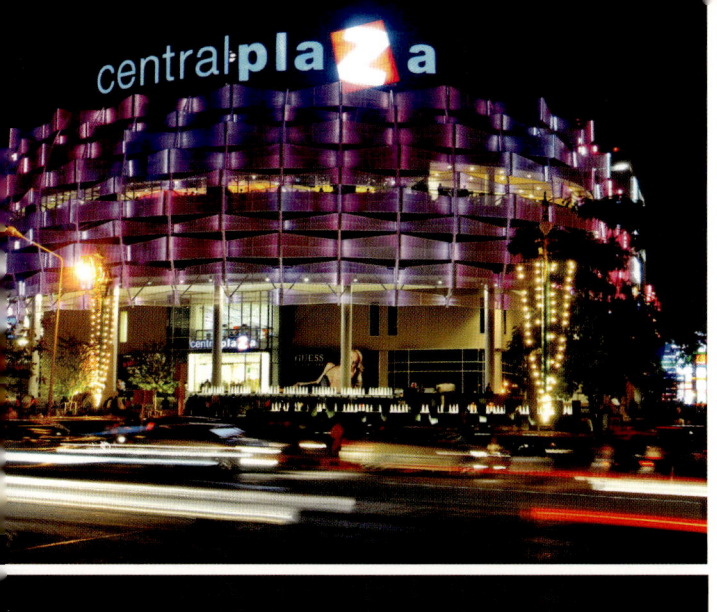

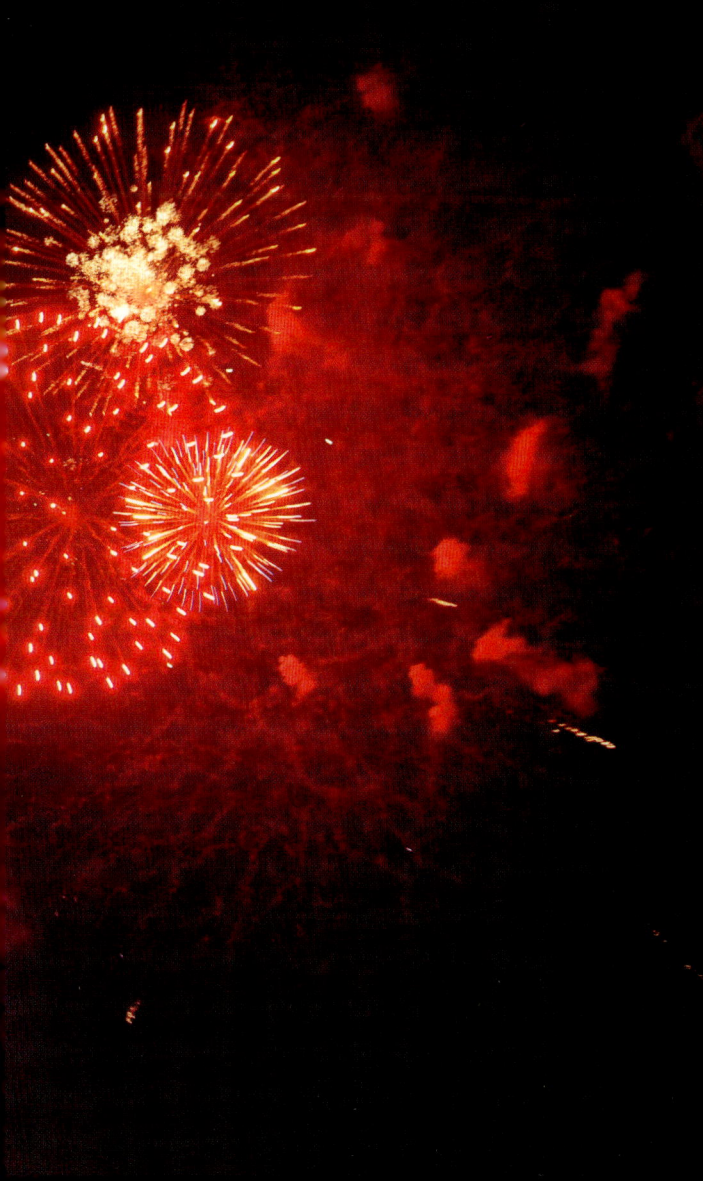

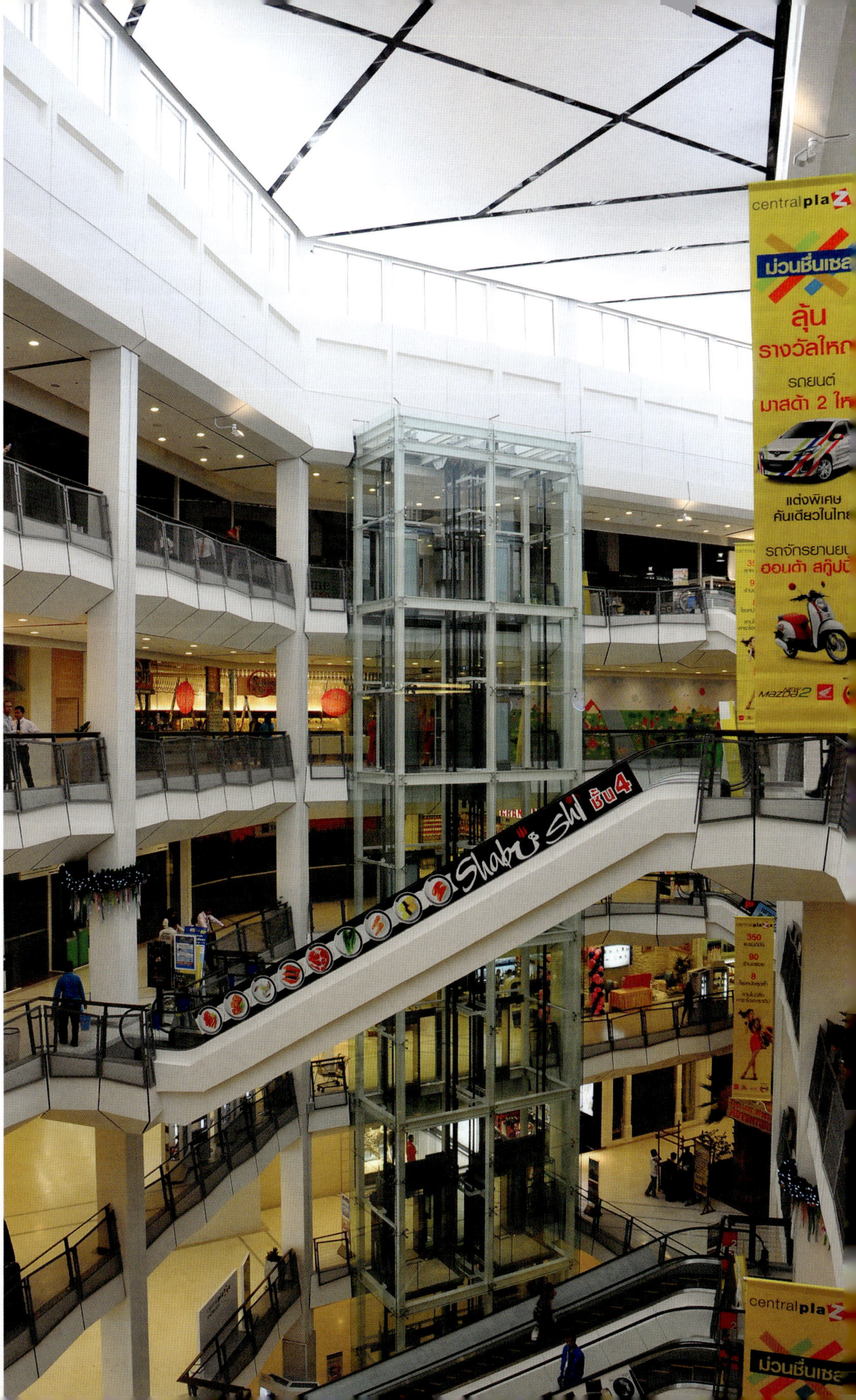
Shabu Shi ชั้น4
ลุ้น
รถยนต์

009

The 49 Terrace   Architects 49

Location :	**Client :**	**Area :** **Year :**
Sukhumvit 49, Bangkok	The 49 Terrace	1,885 sq.m. 2003-2005

A small neighborhood retail facility serving an upscale residential area, 49 Terrace is a charming community hub where people meet and shop. Three levels of retail shops and outdoor terraces surround a tree-lined central opening court. Visual connection with the half-level connecting stairs provides unimpeded customer access to the retail outlets on the higher floor – all shops are clearly seen from the central courtyard space. Multiple open spaces integrate with simple yet well-proportioned architecture. Existing and newly-planted trees are incorporated into the design to preserve a degree of transparency while projecting a screen-like quality from the street.

Central courtyard space links all retail levels.

Central court space at night.

010

Siam **Paragon** Shopping Center

Design 103 International

Location :
Pathum Wan, Bangkok

Client :
Siam Paragon Development

Area :
422,536 sq.m.

Year :
2002- 2005

Siam Paragon, 'the Pride of Bangkok', is the first luxurious shopping complex in Thailand offering world-class international brand products and various entertainment services. The designer's aim is to create an exceptionally upscale one-stop shopping center for local and foreign consumers.

The complex offers a variety of retail stores, restaurants, multiplex movie theaters, an exhibition hall and the Siam Ocean World aquarium - the largest aquarium in South East Asia.

The glass facade details create an abstract installation which entrances customers with its unique design. The vertical garden entrance becomes an appealing focal point; fascinating shoppers with its delicate details. The public space comes to life with the rhythmic pattern of the over-lapping escalators. The cavernous center space affords optimum views from every floor serving the event organizing area. Intermingling practical function and elaborate design, Siam Paragon received the International Council of Shopping Center's (ICSC) 2007 Innovative Design and Development of a New Project award.

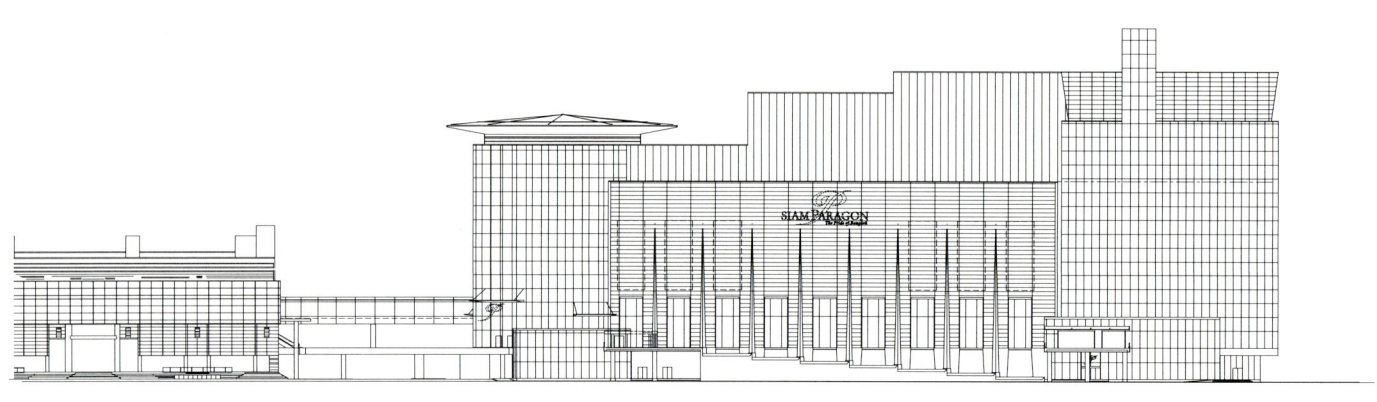

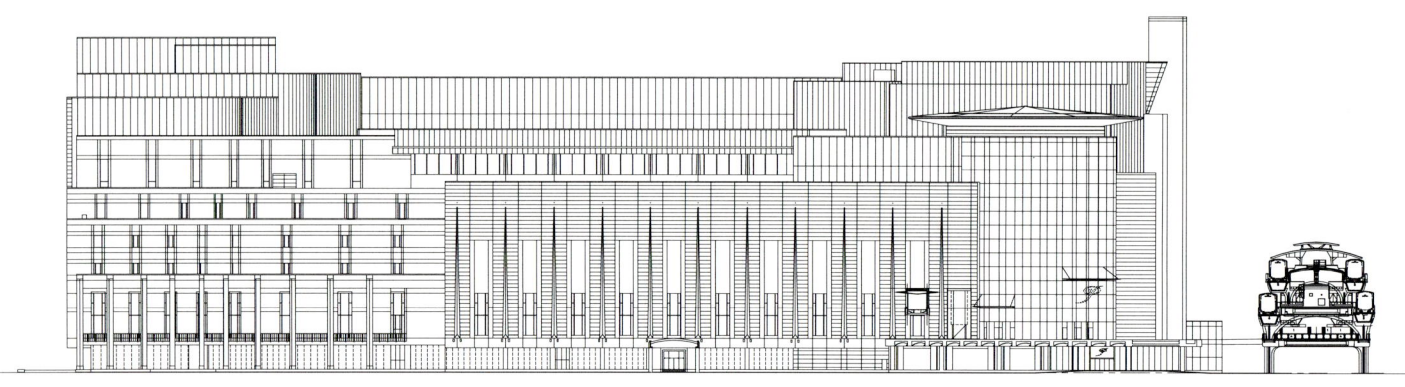

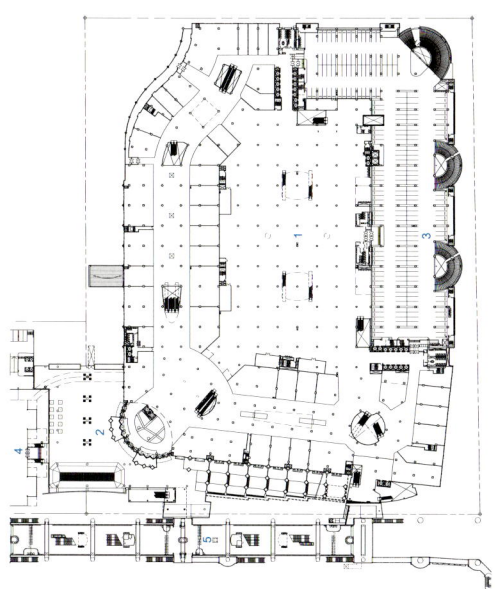

011

Uawithya Showroom   dwp

Location : Saraburi   **Client :** Uawithya Machinery   **Area :** 585 sq.m.   **Year :** 2005-2006

Uawithya is a highly successful Thai business specializing in the sale of large high-quality German and French quarry and mining equipment.

The project's goal was to create a new industry archetype that could be easily built by contractors in diverse locations across Thailand. The showroom, a unique Mitrphap Road landmark, features a two-story double-height external awning that covers large equipment in front of the building. The aesthetics are "modern industrial, extensively employing steel and glass. Inside, the showroom celebrates every day industry products and features an exposition area showcasing new goods and mining methods. The intention is to create a new industry service and design bench mark; with many products costing hundreds of thousands of dollars there is a strong case for creating a fun, modern sales and service center.

Mimicking the main architecture, an open and transparent design concept was adopted for the retail space and interior. Emphasizing open space and easy product access, the designer introduced a new concept to the oversized industrial and machinery product retail environment.

The key retail exhibits concept was derived from the industrial gallery and exhibition hall. Instead of displaying products in common vignettes, the exhibition format enhances the customer's product exposure and education. The design avoids overcrowded displays, leaving walking space around each item. Multimedia and information board juxtaposing offer a multi-sensory experience rarely seen in industrial showrooms.

The polished concrete ground floor and upper viva board combine with raw, natural material colors to create a bright, warm and welcoming atmosphere. The structure's white frame and neutral colors emphasize the client's graphics and colorful merchandise.

Surrounded by all glass walls and immersive specialty lighting, the showroom items are externally visible from a distance, especially at night when the building is lit.

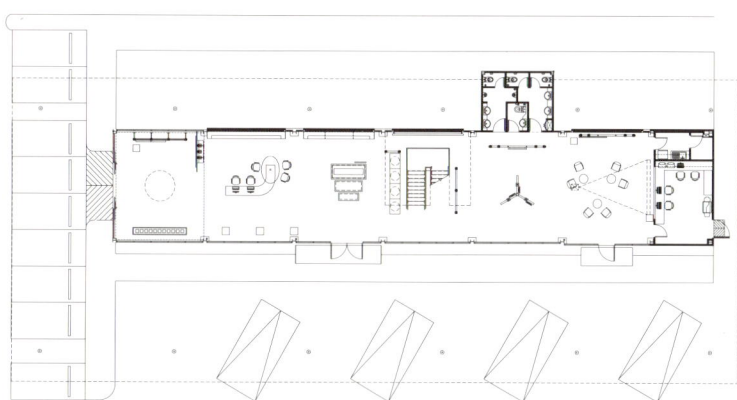

3 layers of roof structure.

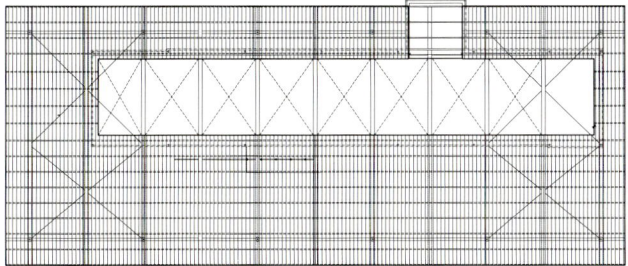

Level 3

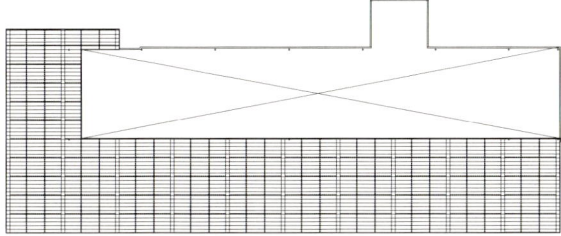

Level 2

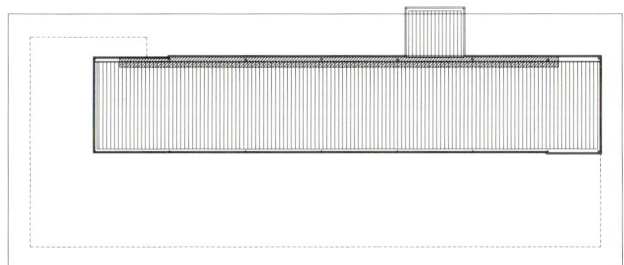

Level 1

012

Workpoint Studio Village   Form Architect

Location :	Client :	Area :	Year :
Pathum Thani	Workpoint Entertainment	31,390 sq.m.	2005-2007

Workpoint Entertainment is the largest TV studio in Thailand. It is one of the top studios in Asia, producing all types of television shows, advertisements, songs, soap operas and movies. The locale, once known for rice cultivation, has been developed into residential and commercial zones. The concept was to synchronize the agricultural granaries with a modern industrial entertainment complex.

The heart of the Entertainment Industry Village is the TV program producers and participants. The Village's unique architectural style provides inspiration and creativity for producers, while the convenient amenities and friendly environment ensure the TV show participants' comfort. This inspiration and comfort promote cooperation between the parties and result in knowledgeable and entertaining TV programming.

With a location based on Feng Shui principles, the design concept was to create an architectural work that reflects the unique local identity, spirit and way of life through its connection with irrigation, rice cultivation and fishing. The front and ground-level court circulates water into the building, symbolizing fortune, movement, growth and progress. Rice is represented through the granary-inspired design symbolizing stability, centrality, abundance, power and success. Both symbols are covered by a large roof reminiscent of a 'yok-yor' - fisherman's net - symbolizing unity and harmony. The roof is aptly themed 'architectural handicraft/weave engineering' or 'Shade and shadow decorating'. The overall design reflects Workpoint's 'To work together towards the success point' motto.

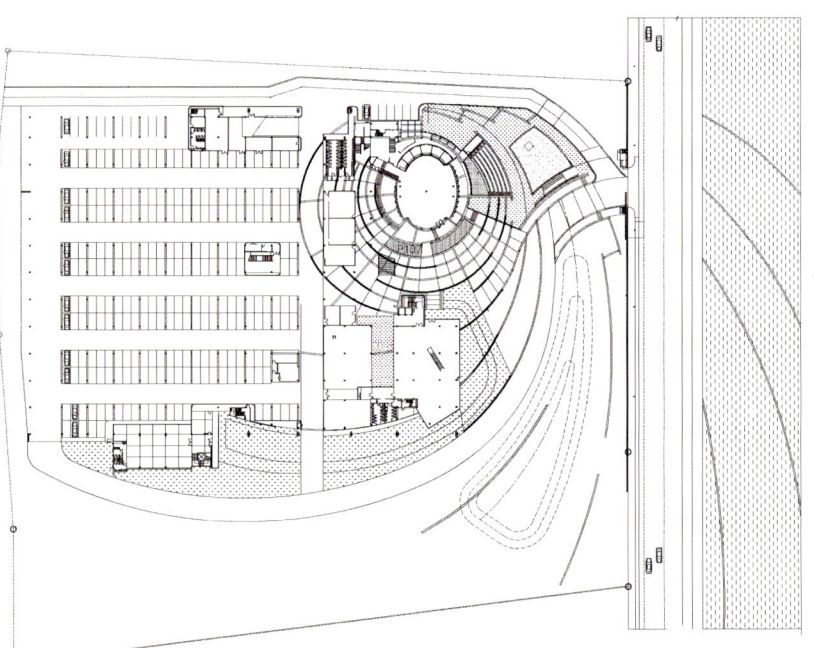

Inner garden court in the heart. Creates a relaxing atmosphere for the office zone.

Sky lounge at third floor.

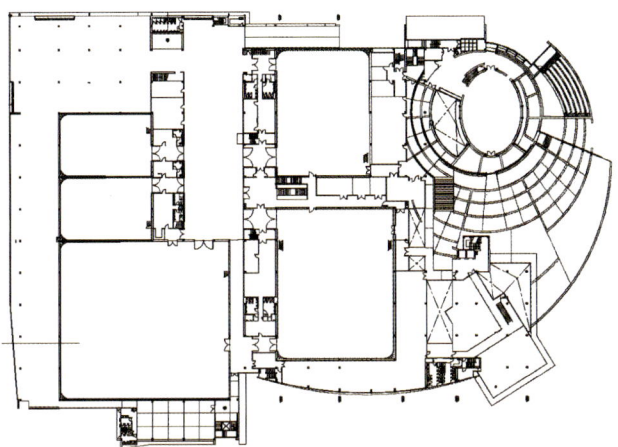

2nd floor plan

013

Amari Residences Hua Hin Street Side Restaurant
Great Architect

Location :	**Client :**	**Area :**
Hua Hin, Prachuap Khiri Khan	Amari Hua Hin	918 sq.m.
		Year :
		2009

The Amari Residences Hua Hin's Street Side Restaurant is located in the beautiful seaside city of 'Hua Hin'. The design expresses a wavy, peaceful ethos translated into the concrete. The varied depth of the GRC wall produces the building's daytime shading variation while hidden GRC lighting gives the structure a shimmering, soft nocturnal glow.

N

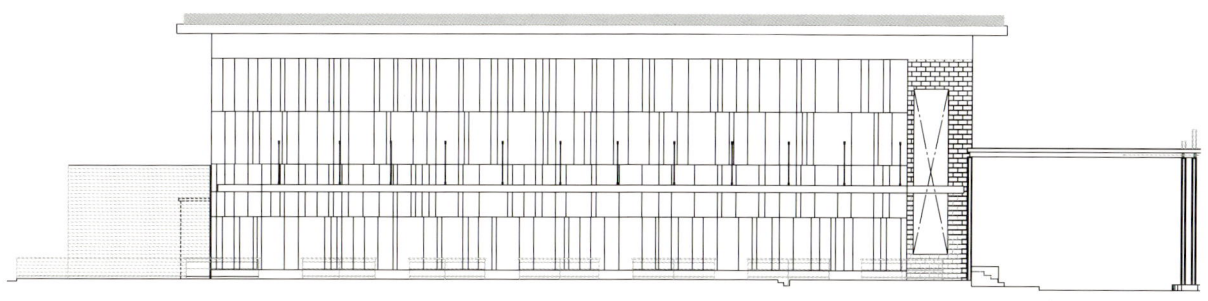

Unexampled GRC wall with lighting illuminated around the facade.

Mock-up room

014

Practika Factory   Plan Associates

Location :
Rattanakosin Somphote Road, Bangkok

Client :   Practika

Area :   10,000 sq.m.

Year :   2004–2007

Practika Factory designs and produces furniture under the brand name 'Practika'. The conceptual design of the Practika Factory tackles the challenge of creating a factory that physically and psychologically interacts its internal staff and external environment. The relationship between the workers and their environment is factored in so as to enhance the employee's quality of life.

The factory's architectural design expresses a modern, dynamic furniture industry image. The design also identifies the plant's quality identity; which is the most important commercial aspect.

The project plan addresses the building functionality simply and directly. Understanding furniture mass production is the key to creating a successful strategy. The position of the machines, the traffic area and control system are clearly designed to maximizing the use of space while providing manufacturing flexibility.

The elongated 3-story factory is covered by a giant curved metal panel and overlapping louver panel which creates a consistency in the structure's shade and shadow. The louver provides ventilation as well as an open view from inside. This combination of curved metal panel, louver and the green spatial surroundings creates a unique factory appearance.

N

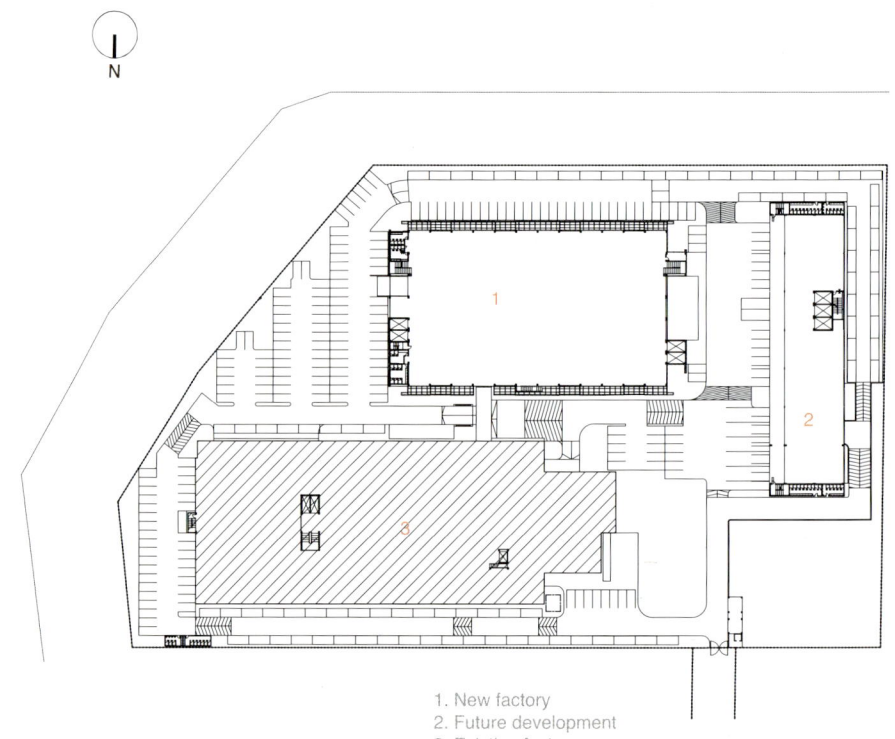

1. New factory
2. Future development
3. Existing factory

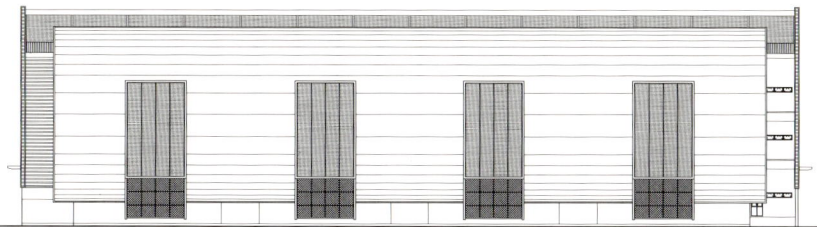

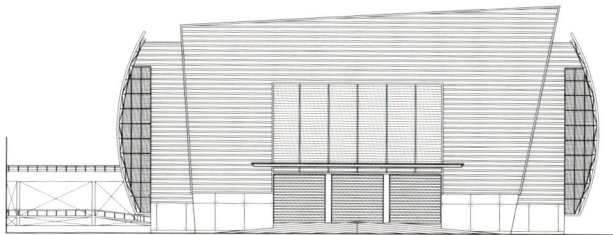

Dust silo structure

Exterior of the silo

Linkage between new and existing factory

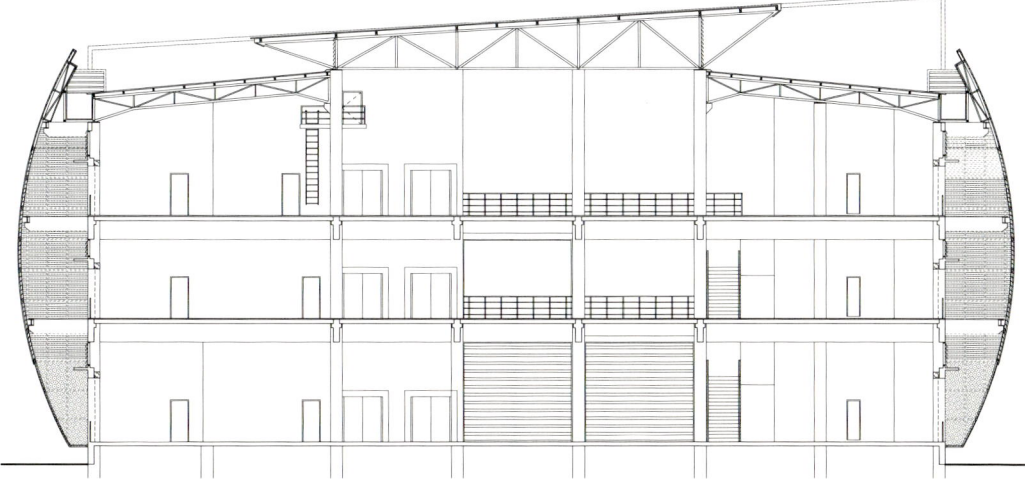

Curved facade structure

015

Maze Plankrich

Location :
Boonreungrit, Sripoom, Muang, Chiang Mai

Client :
Tanit Choomsang

Area :
460 sq.m.

Year :
2007

"How can a restaurant encourage the blossoming of community participation?"

This question is the key to the cool, hip Maze Café restaurant design. Unlike for other restaurants by the Chiang Mai city moat, the goal for the Maze is to integrate and participate with the community. Thus, heavy fencing at the main entrance is replaced by open space that is used to host significant local festival events and activities such as Song-kran. With large trees providing event shading, the front terrace is a perfect place for the city's festival celebrations.

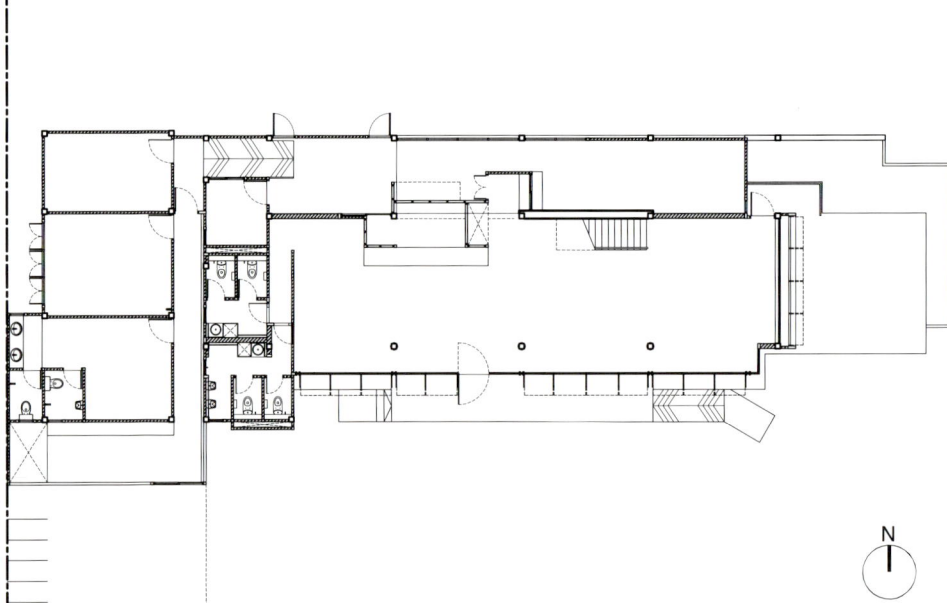

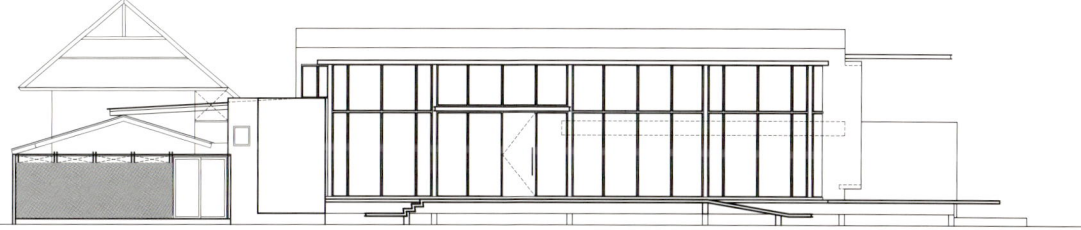

Location :
Laem Chabang, Chon Buri

Client : Prakit Chaisongkram

Area : 500 sq.m.

Year : 2008-2010

016

Harbormall   Supermachine Studio

Laemtong Shopping mall, Laemchabang, is one thousands of Thai projects heavily affected by the 1997 Asian economy crisis. The 100,000 square meter Laemtong Shopping mall was half-empty and declining. The high rise section was decaying and the building was architecturally worn.

The structural renovation started in 2007, ten years after crisis, under a new name, Harbormall. An aggressively budgeted plan for its size, the design includes a facade and front plaza redesign and a new interior to suit the location's new business landscape.

The facade is an all-new steel structure covering the face of the old building. The new skin, attached to steel frames, is composed of some 2,000 pieces laminated glass fins with 7 different customized colors. With the multi-layering of transparent materials, the gap between the old and the new facade adds complex lucidity to building. It turns from a giant blue box during the day to a glowing green one in the evening. The aim of the new shopping mall design is to reveal more interior pedestrian movement rather than employ conventional solid wall architecture.

The inner shopping mall has been through an extensive transformation process. More natural light is brought into the space via a large skylight. In addition, simple, clean and light elements were selected to supplant extravagant legacy materials.

New steel structure facade covering the old building.

Facade composed with 2,000 pieces laminated glass with 7 different colors.

017

Esplanade & Ratchadalai Theater

The Office of Bangkok Architects

Location :
Ratchadaphisek Road, Bangkok

Client :
Siam Future Development

Area :
100,000 sq.m.

Year :
2005-2007

Situated adjacent to the Thailand Cultural Center subway station, The Esplanade shopping center comprises six floors with a basement level. Its tenants include a supermarket, restaurants, retail shops, 24-lane bowling, 12 cinemas, an ice rink, a fitness center, a 1,500-seat theater and a 10-level, 800-car parking garage.

The building' s design concept is built around the Seven Arts themes - architecture, music, sculpture, painting, poetry, performing art and celluloid art. With a simple massing profile, the building has been designed with a modern glass facade and a flowing, curvilinear roof to achieve a unique 'lifestyle' architecture that is true to the buildings 'arte-tainment' concept.

In designing the building's floor plan, the main entry was positioned near the entrance to the subway station, while two secondary valet parking entries were provided as a central point to the building's core. The five-level glass facade allows natural light to penetrate deep into the structure and creates a distinct connection to the 'green space'; a natural setting of timber and stone paving landscaped with plants and water pools that encircles the building.

The striking central atrium connects directly to the main entrance. Designed to create a dynamic voluminous space, the atrium creates an illusionary effect with its varying void profiles and discordant leaning columns. A mezzanine level adjuncts the ground floor open event area and is accessed through a translucent staircase with glazed treads. Together with the building-in-building facade design and the continuation of the timber terrace and pond from outside, an outdoor atmosphere within an enclosed mall was created.

The principal interior spaces were designed with a French-based design firm. The restaurant orientated basement level follows a different design concept from the upper levels. While it features an open ceiling, the upper floors feature a web of diamond formation coved lighting that assists with creating the internal architectures' disorientating nature. The glass railings around the voids are themselves angled to follow the ceiling formation.

Indoor landscape at ground level.

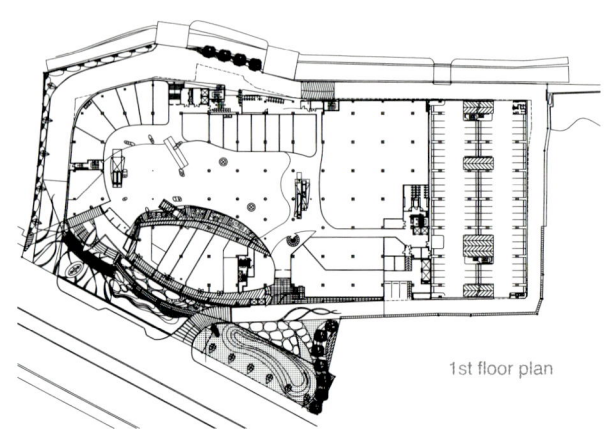

1st floor plan

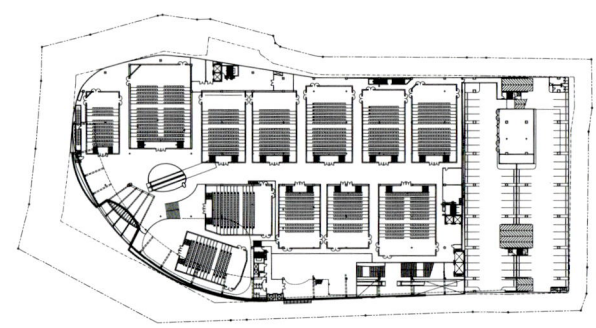

2nd floor plan

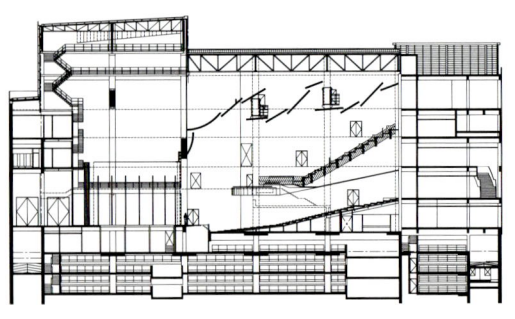

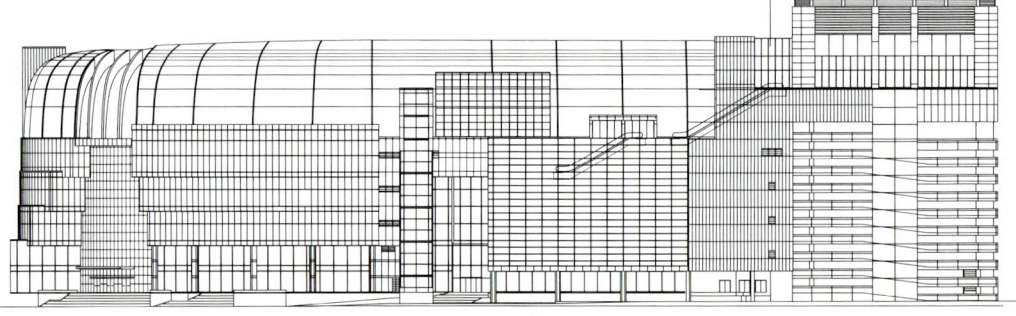

Ratchadalai theater:
Auditorium wall pattern resemble to thai "Pha Pragon Wall".

018

K Village   The Office of Bangkok Architects

Location :
Sukhumvit 26 Road, Bangkok

Client :
Kananan

Area :
14,000 sq.m.

Year :
2009

The architectural design utilizes the intertwining range of varying curvilinear and rectangular building masses to create two distinct courtyards, each providing multiple access points to the retail shops. Natural elements are integrated throughout both buildings, seamlessly connecting the outside and inside while emphasizing the outdoor rectilinear and elliptical event courtyards. The landscaping and water features adjoining the architectural spaces elevate the customer experience for both shoppers and diners. The intention was to create a backdrop of white and light grey through the center's walls and floors to accentuate the lush landscaping and the diverse array of shop fronts.

The external facade is created from the subtle transformation of a series of twisted volumes. Constructed from individual I-beams and finished with decorative timber paneling, the structure suggests an implied facade that creates a unique and dynamic external elevation along the centre's street front. The internal stairs and balustrades of each building present distinctive forms and characteristics, yet suggest an underlying coherence when viewed as a whole. These architectural interventions, together with the dynamic interiors and landscape features, create varied perspectives, ensuring each visit brings with it a new experience and perception of the mall.

The center provides a stylish and chic meeting place with approximately 80 retail shops, 50 small store fronts, an office and approximately 300 parking spaces. The tenant mix includes fashion and beauty stores, restaurants offering a range of cuisines, as well as a supermarket.

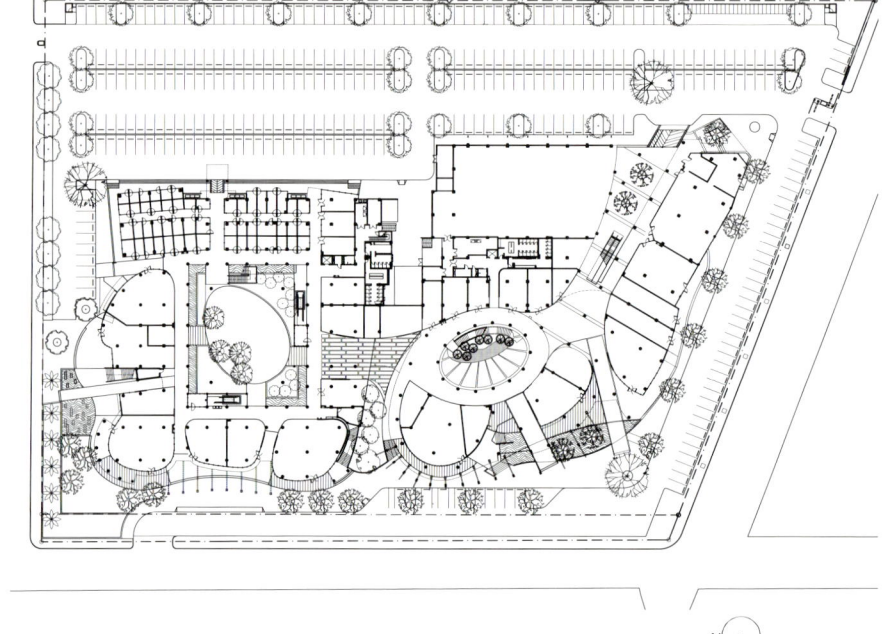

N

Sun shaded structure creats a unique and dynamic effect.

019

Mini Showroom

The Office of Bangkok Architects

Location : Ekamai Road, Bangkok

Client : Millennium Auto

Area : 6,000 sq.m.

Year : 2006-2007

The architectural and interior design concept of the Mini Showroom was inspired by the prominent graphic forms expressed in Bauhaus architecture. The showroom itself provides for up to 18 vehicles and includes customer services and administrative office space. To accommodate the needs of Mini devotees, a lifestyle and leisure club was provided for owners to meet and share their mutual appreciation of the Mini.

The industrial articulation of the building architecture has been refined through sophisticated construction methodologies and materiality. With this new venture, Mini has targeted a new generation, appreciative of creative aspects of art, design and the theater. It was Mini's aim to create an environment that would reflect both the company's brand along with their new target market. Another important conceptual element was the clients' intention to showcase the cars within a 'display box' platform. To achieve this, the architects have created a series of volumetric frameworks, finished with LED lighting to emphasize the cars. Internally, the design reflects the buildings external structure with the use of steel and mesh paneling. Prominent matt black finishes provide a stylish backdrop, with highly focused lighting showcasing the classic aesthetic of the Mini.

With an open brief, the building's constraint was the construction cost to conform to local steel structure fire safety regulatory ordinances. In response, the architects opted to express the architectural language on only the frontal part of the showroom facade with an expressed metal framework and glazed curtain wall. Steel Structure and glazed panel flooring were designed only for the showroom on the first 2-levels, while the remaining elements are constructed from post-tensioned concrete slab, an inexpensive alternative that enabled the building to be contained within prevailing height limits of 23 meters. The site constraints also made ramps problematic, so internal car parking and maintenance workshops are all accessed through two purpose-built car elevators.

Front facade

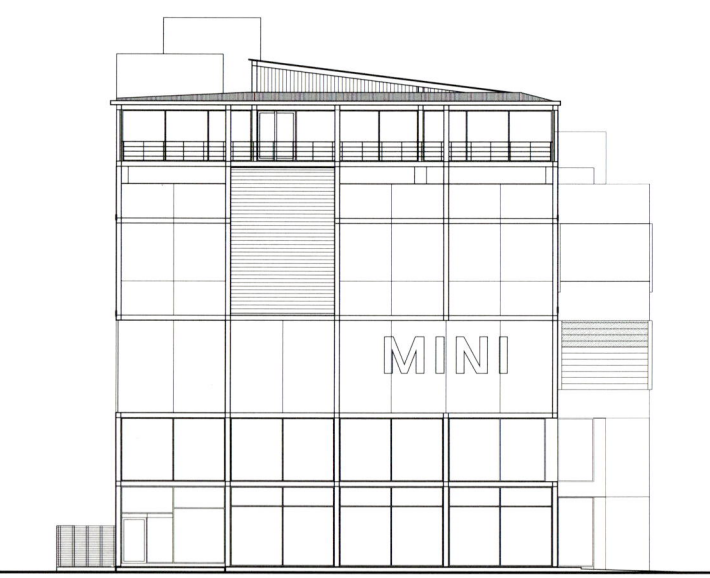

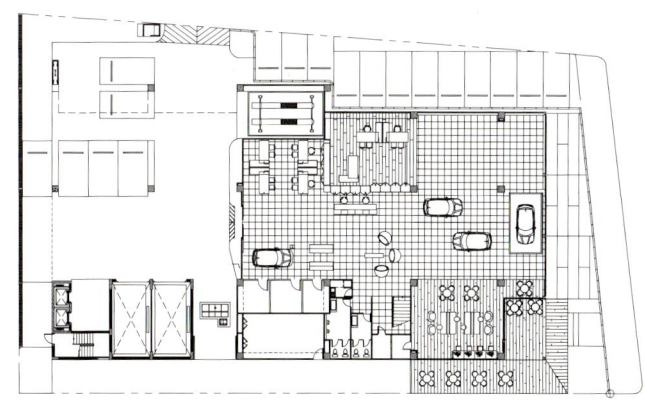

The opening above the showroom area

Honda Big Wing VaSLab

Location :
Pradit Manutham Road, Bangkok

Client :
AP Honda

Area :
2,300 sq.m.

Year :
2007-2009

This Honda Big Wing showroom is a competition winning project awarded in September 2007. The client's project was selected to be the first big-bike center in Asia Pacific, reinforcing the manufacturer's brand and serving as the destination of choice for a nearby community.

This new Bangkok leader brings in many low-rise commercial projects as magnets for recreation and leisure. The fast traffic speed became the force fluctuated in and out the site to create zoning formation.

The design proposal caught the client's attention with its metaphorical plan that articulates Honda's "attitude of winning" slogan. Not only is the design functional, but it evokes the corporate identity.

Imposing sculptural concrete forms, inspired by the 'hugging the curve' transition, convey the winning moment of motorcycle racing. The two boomerangs engage one another in plans and sections. The first guides its circulation from main entry through the café, showroom, retail shop, education zone, and warehouse. The other directs its flow through the lounge and conference area via offices, the canteen, service center and workshop. The triangle site's open space hugged by these boomerangs becomes the test track.

The use of eco-friendly concrete is applied throughout the project. Its masculine finishes flows outside-in as seen from the continuous exterior surface and interior wall and ceiling. The fluid interior circulation is designed to follow the same dynamic characteristic of its outer shell.

Front display area to workshop at ground level.

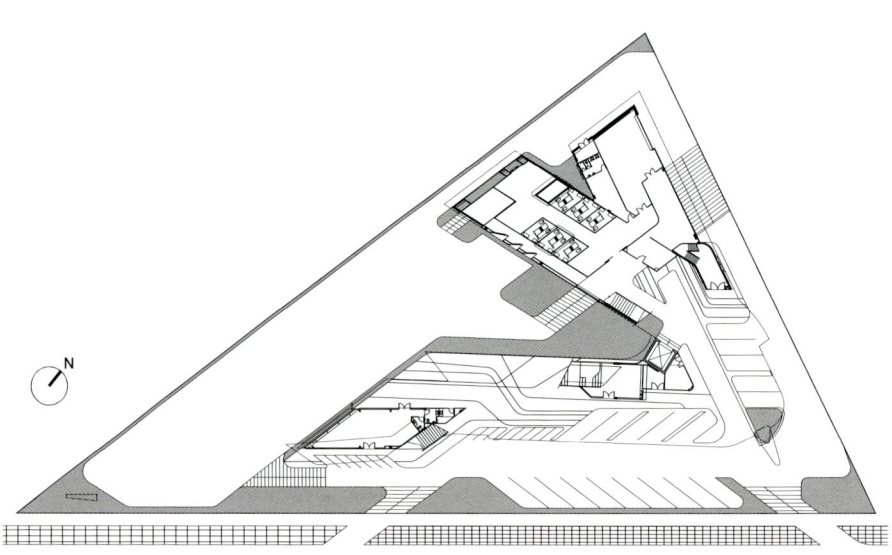

N

The two boomerang-like forms interest each other, representing the concept of "the overtaking forms".

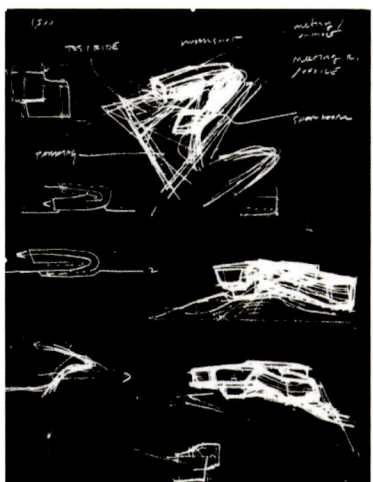

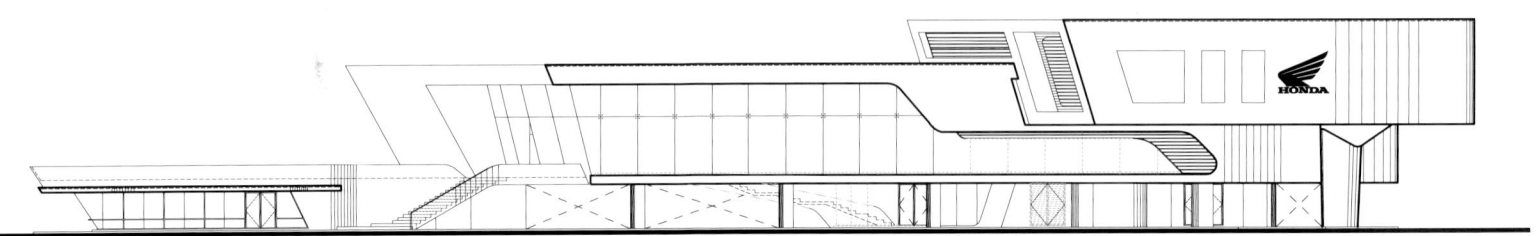

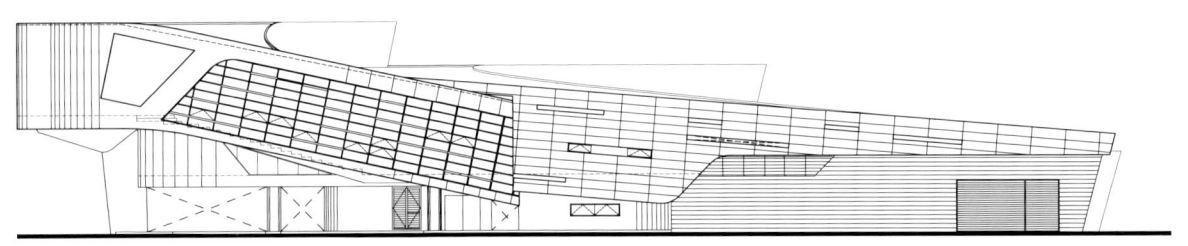

The stair to mezzanine level, tunnel structural design.

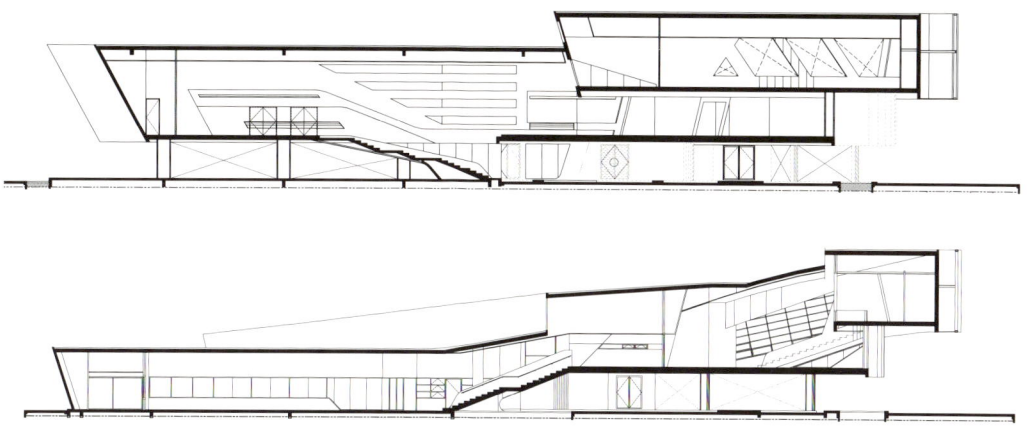

021

Chai Tour Office

amA design studio

Location :
Narathiwas Rajanakarindra Road, Bangkok

Client :
Chai Tour

Area :
1,020 sq.m.

Year :
2005-2009

The 4-story tour office was constructed following the owner's philosophy that a building's architecture should reflect a positive image for the organization. Natural air and lightning were used to showcase this concept and reduce air conditioning use. The idea was to design a building that would breathe on its own. Large interior spaces were created, including an inside open air courtyard that ventilates naturally during the hot season. Dense, natural stone walls direct airflow throughout the building, and perforated, stained glass corridors maintain a relaxed, airy feel. Laminated privacy glass walls add a sense of interior openness.

The ground floor reception hall and dining room welcome visitor openly. It is a cavernous space surrounded with a garden and pond. The high ceiling is designed to improve air flow to every floor and create a cozier environment. The front building was designed in 5 meter cantilever from the main structure to lighten the building. The lower area provides flexible support to daytime and nighttime activities. The roof has a standing canopy to reduce sunlight and minimize the building's presence.

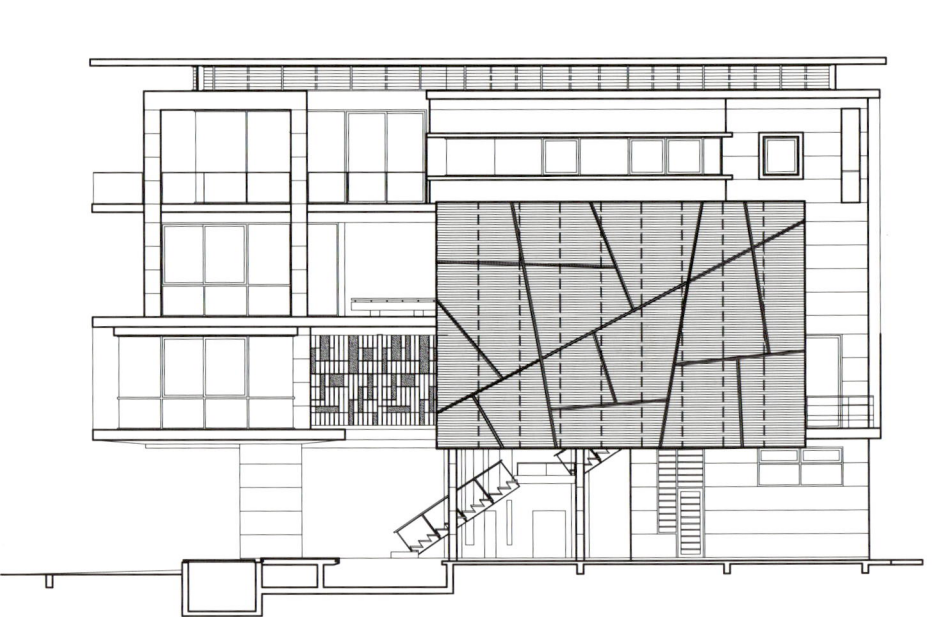

Pattern wooden screen reduces solar glare for executive room and blend the building to the surrounding.

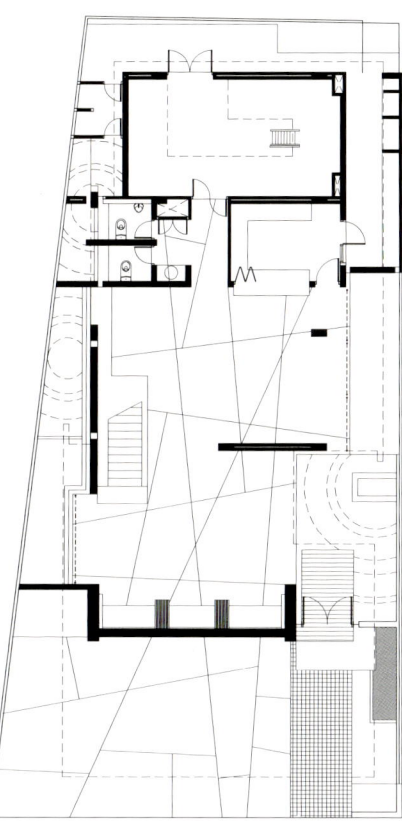

| 1 | 2 |

1. Wooden roof top pattern
2. Pattern breathed wall

022

Architect Council of Thailand
ARbay / Krisda Panitkosol

Location :
Rama IX Road, Bang Kapi, Bangkok

Client :
Architect Council of Thailand

Area :
2,000 sq.m.

Year :
2008-2010

The creation of architecture, that provides usable space function, creates aesthetic value, quality of life and also architecture symbolic, is the outcomes from the thoughtful imagination of architect.

Comparing to a tree, if we turn it upside down, we will clearly see that the origin of a tree is its root. In the process of creation architecture, an architect represents an important root, the root of thinking that collects experiences, imaginations and feelings.

This idea is the main design concept that is aimed to present the importance of those architects who are the root of thinking, who expand their thought through generations of young architects.
'CITY OF SPACE', another main design concept of ACT building, is the idea that reflects architecture as a place where all groups of architecture-related professions are gathered. The building itself is the combination of various forms of building mass. Each masses have their own identities and all of them are linked to each other by walk way and circulation.

ACT is the organization that provides social service related to all architecture professions. A warm welcoming building design with open space retains a strong connection with the outside and surrounding elements of the town.

A material selection of glass wall depends on different functions. The silver-gray glass wall is utilized in an office area while the golden yellow glass is used in a media room.

A circulation of space which is identical to the concept of a traditional Thai house formulates the connection from outside to inside. The wide open link between ground floor to the second and third floor forms a unique feature of the building.

A large curvy roof covering the main conference room and other functions.

A pre-function hall prior to the conference room serve both as an exhibition space and reception area.

A wavy stairs rising connecting all spaces together as well as drawing predestrain traffic into the building.

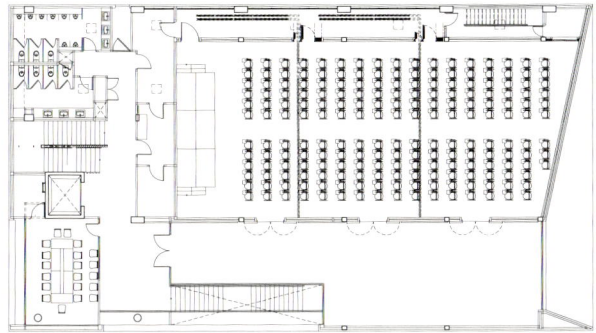

3rd floor plan

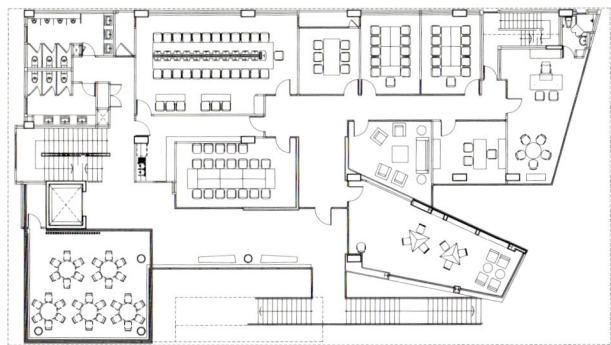

2nd floor plan

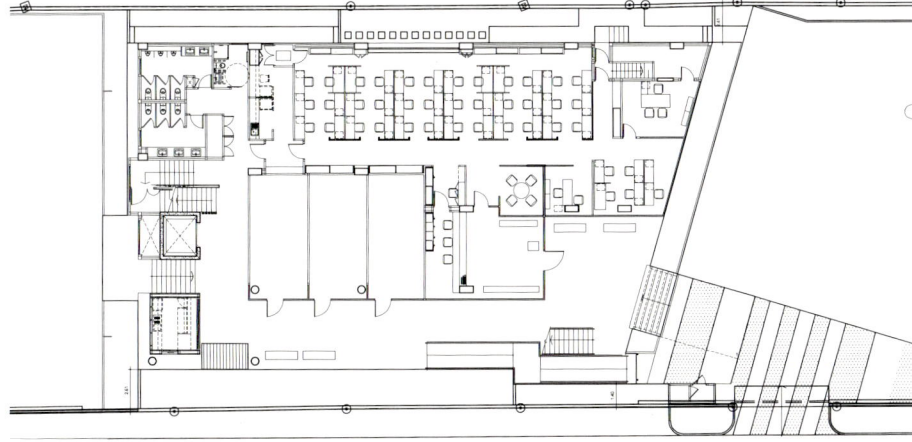

1st floor plan

023

Energy Complex

Architects 49 / Design Concept

Location :
Vibhavadi Rangsit Road, Bangkok

Client :
Energy Complex Group

Area :
177,000 sq.m.

Year :
2004-2009

Serving not only as the headquarters of the Ministry of Energy, but also of the Petroleum Authority of Thailand (PTT), the Energy Complex's architectural design and engineering were intended to be a distinctive model of energy conservation for other large building to emulate.

After painstaking consultation with engineers and energy conservation experts, and consideration of multiple design options, two concepts were submitted. The strict energy conservation constraints required careful consideration of the choice of exterior wall covering and the use of multi-layered windows.

The middle zone was included to connect the PTT with the Ministry and to provide access to a shared auditorium, library and recreational area.

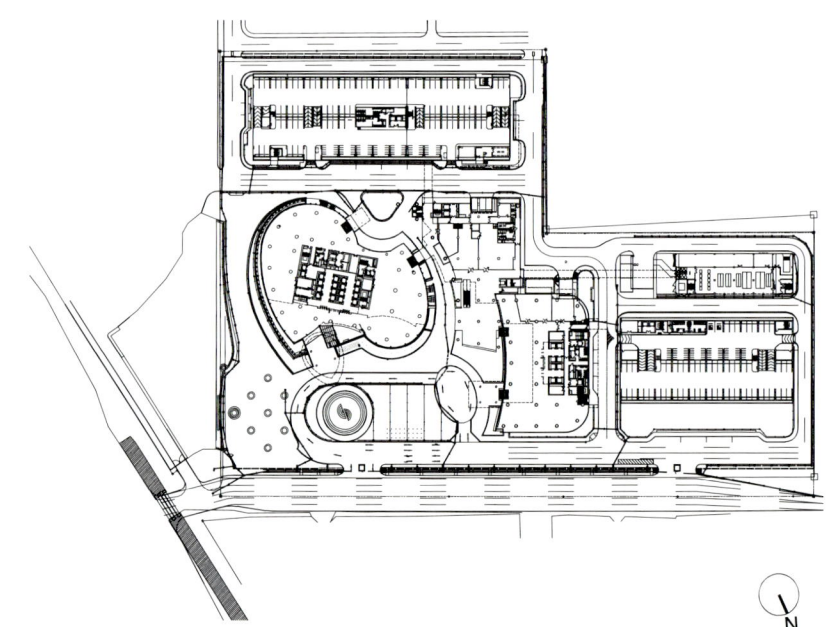

N

Concepts were shape of a drop of oil, the exterior wall
covering and the use of multi-layered windows.

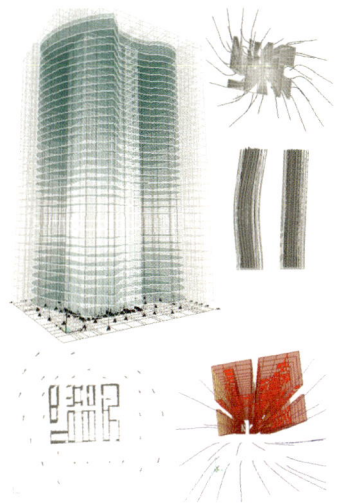

Finite element analysis

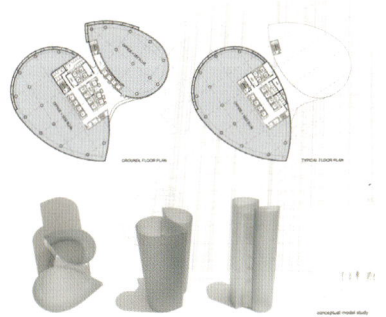

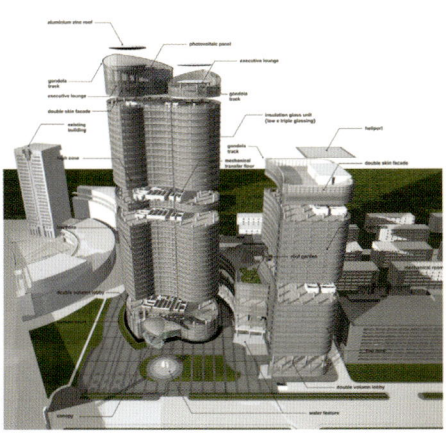

The main entrance of Tower B

024

Royal Archive

Architects 49

Location :
Putthamonthon Road, Nakhon Pathom

Client :
The Office of His Majesty's Principal Private Secretary

Area : 17,653 sq.m.

Year : 2006-2009

As the principal office of his Majesty's private secretary's resource center, the Royal Archive Center collects and provides access to Chakri-dynasty historical artifacts. The center consists of 13,179 square meters of storage area, 1,000 square meters of exhibition, library and conference areas, an information service center and a rentable archival storage space.

Zone clarity is the important aspect of this design. The two-story front exhibition hall's hanging roof serves as an entrance to the project, followed by the 3-story library and the rear five-story archive building. All parking is underground.

The design pursues contemporary modern architecture while blending a Thai essence into the details. Since the archive houses priceless documents, manuscripts, engravings and photographs, the humidity, temperature and lighting control are paramount considerations.

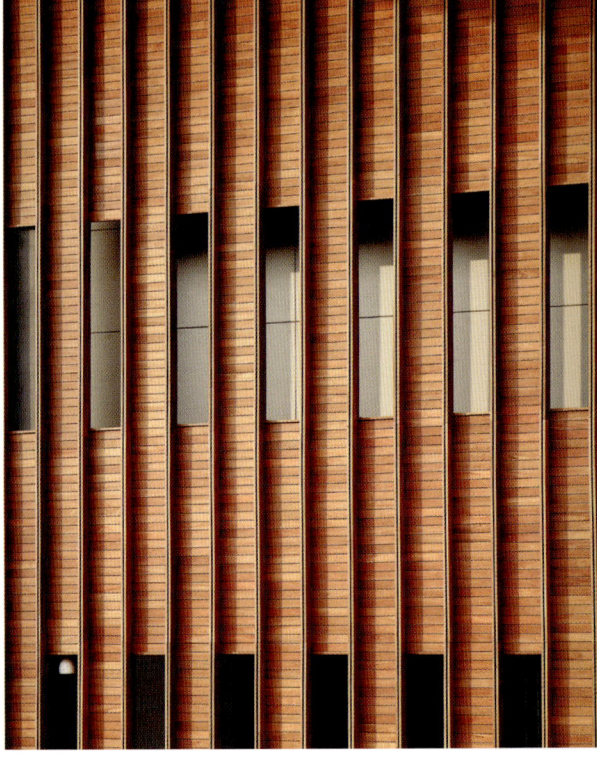

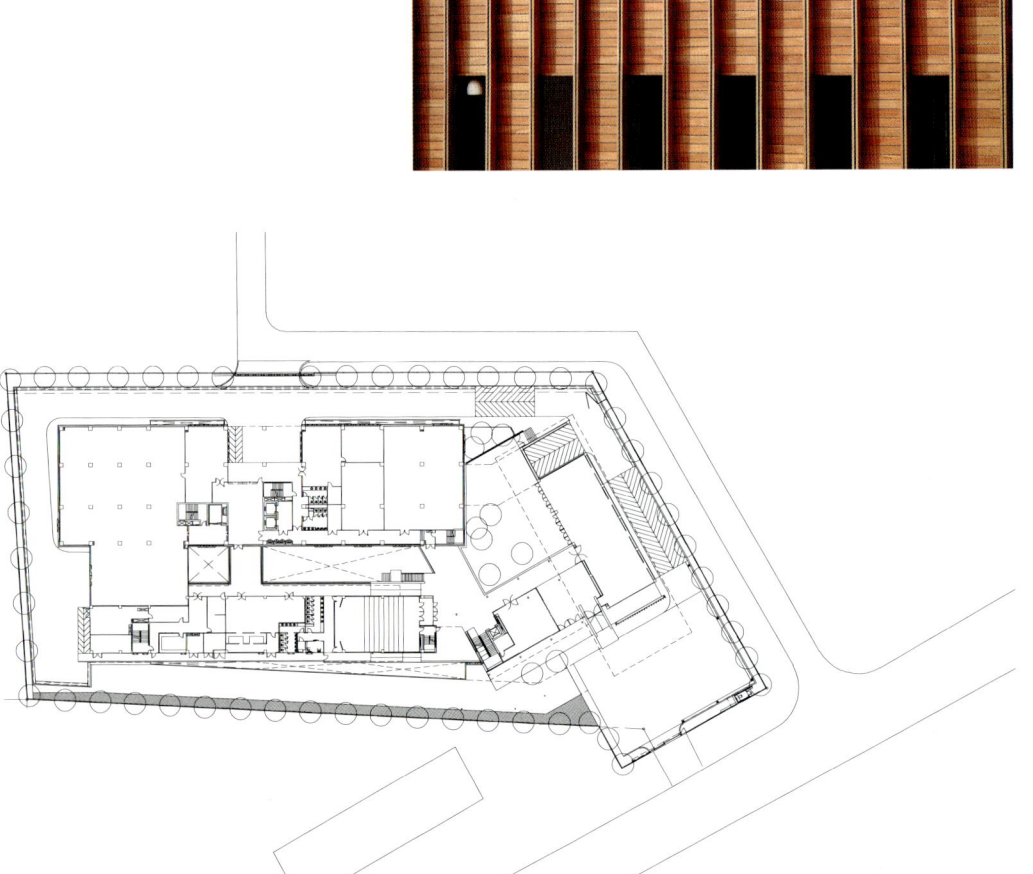

Main entrance

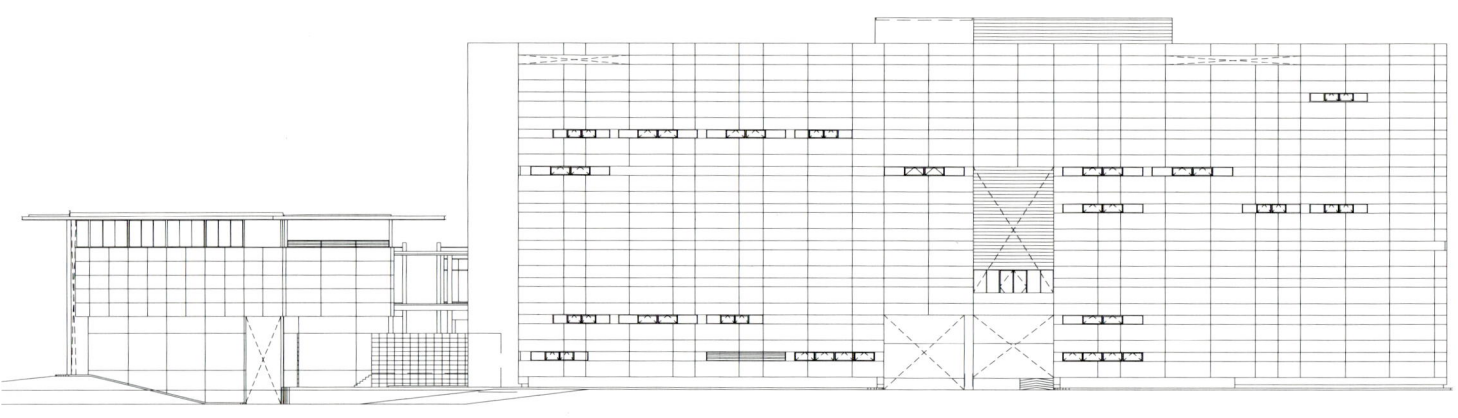

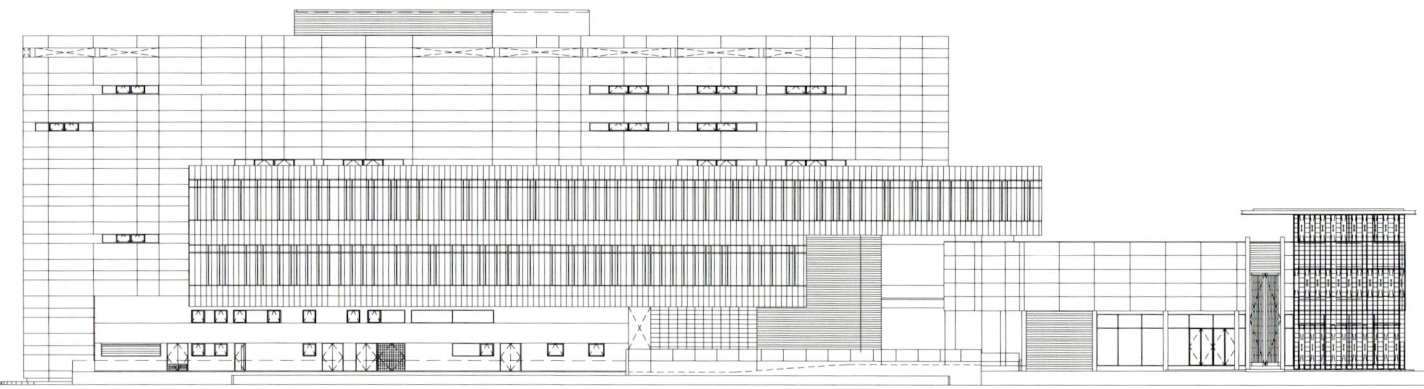

025

Crew Training Center (Renovation)

Architects & Associates

Location :
Vibhavadi Rangsit Road, Lak Si, Bangkok

Client :
Thai Airways International

Area : 3,000 sq.m.

Year : 2006-2009

The Reception & Administrative Office Building was built in 1994 in the 1st airport project phase, but it was used as a crew terminal center. The originally designed Air Crew Terminal Building was not constructed until the airport was moved to Suvarnabhumi. The building was then converted to office and training rooms.

The first building was built with a limited budget and had been operating for 15 years without some required building features and systems. The renovation project was established not only to improve functionality and interior & exterior architectural appearance, but also to add more safety, security, and energy saving systems. The renovation designs included upgrades to the reception lobby, office and document storage on each floor, various-sized classrooms and training rooms, all toilets, and exterior architectural improvement.

The main design concept was to improve the facility but keep its fundamental nature. The form and line of the building were accented with distinctive dark grey and gold aluminum composite panel composition and the sun shading device was applied to reduce heat gain on west & south façade and create an interesting appearance.

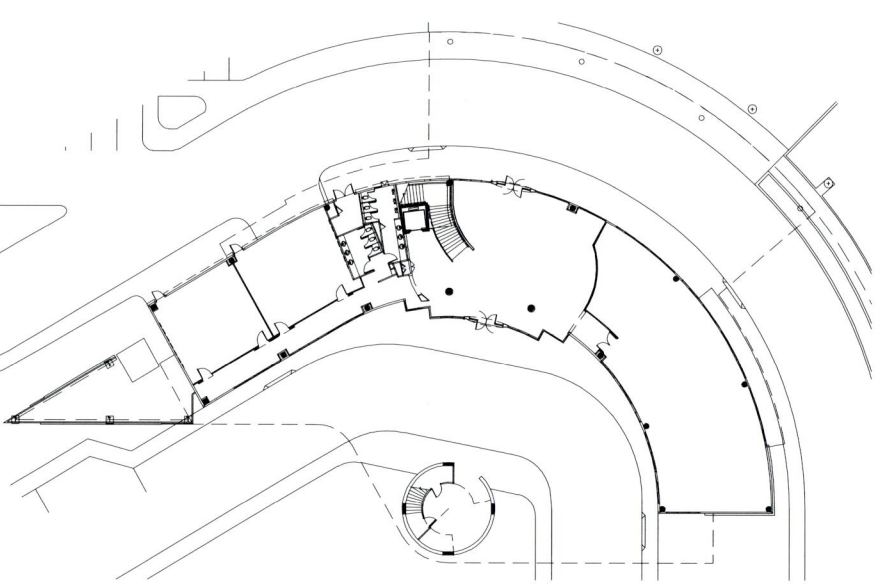

Exterior wall made of aluminum louver concealing
M&E and waste water treament inside.

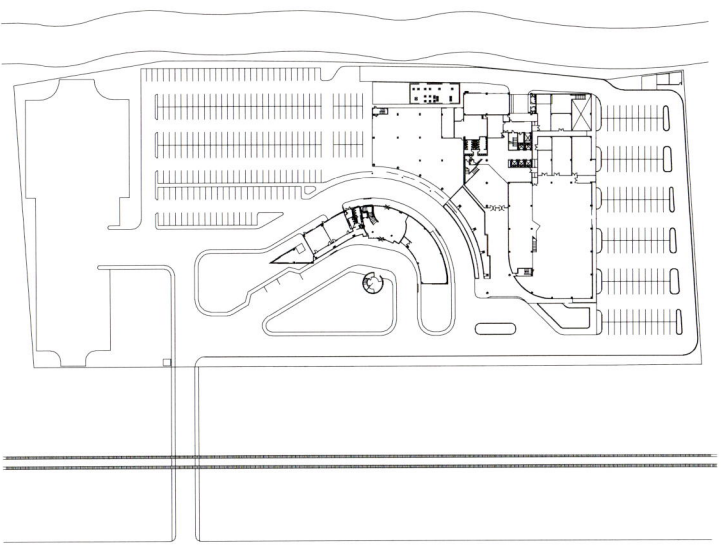

Dynamic form and line of the ceiling in the
entrance lobby.

026

Operation Center

Architects & Associates

Location :
Suvarnabhumi Airport, Samut Prakan

Client :
Thai Airways International

Area :
118,000 sq.m.

Year :
2003-2006

The Operations Center, one of the Thai Airways' PCL Suvarnabhumi Airport projects, is the command center of the other airport projects including the Ground Service Center, Equipment Maintenance Center, Aircraft Maintenance Center, Catering Center, Cargo Center, and the Passenger Terminal Customer Service Center. It is the core of Thai Airways' airport operations.

Simple energy awareness is one of the main design concepts. Most energy savings strategies are incorporated passively to achieve low maintenance costs.

The building is designed to be a unique, modern, and elegant centerpiece of the Thai Airways compound. The structure's orientation optimizes its site location and surrounding view. The building's rectangular form provides practical functional space, rapid construction, and economy. However, the front corner is chamfered along the curved road to create the focal point of the building and enhanced with an elliptical crisis center and operations center over the corner. This area is located at the highest point to provide a panoramic airport view for air traffic control. The curved wall connects the office building and crew center on the other leg of the 'L' shape which surrounds a corner of the rear parking garage. The building's main entrance is distinctively set under the continuous curved line at the corner.

An architectural feature emphasized is the use of modern and low maintenance materials. Blue tint reflective glass is applied to reflect airlines' business identity, while aluminum shading devices and aluminum composite panel are incorporated to accent the solid wall patterns and represent strong organizational development

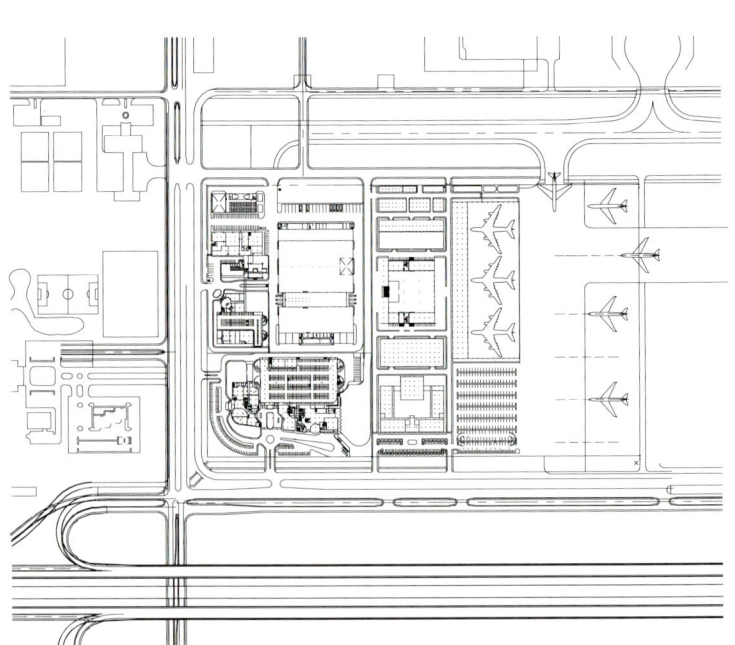

Public entrance of office building lobby.

027

Thailand Elite Head Quarters
Architecture and Interior

Location :
Sathon Road, Bangkok

Client :
Thailand Privilege Card, A subsidiary under the Tourism Authority of Thailand

Area :
1,000 sq.m.

Year :
2004-2005

The Thailand Privilege Card's singular mission is "to condense the very best of Thailand and bring together the best the country has to offer in one package". This corporate vision was the driving force behind the design of their office and reception areas.

The key consideration was to extract elements from traditional Rattana Kosin-style Thai homes and to interpret them into contemporary urban forms that are in sync with international trends.

The 2,000 sq. m. site was previously a worn and nondescript 1970's era, two-story government office. The architect delivered an economical design that transformed the building into a structure with cosmopolitan appeal that preserved the quintessential Thai aesthetic. In a simple but effective move, the facade was given a cosmetic makeover via a full frontal 'timber screen' constructed of acrylic-painted cement boards on steel supports. Its lower portion is chamfered, giving the impression of a high-pitch, inverted-V traditional Thai roof with long eaves skirting its base. Inside, original concrete beams are dressed in teak and the existing retained walls are lined with gold leaf panels framed in steel.

For all its modernity, everything says 'Thai' here, from the Sala-style ceiling right down to the traditional Fa Prakon patterned lounge wall. With skilful lighting, the lounge atmosphere reveals an inviting warmth, comfort and elegance.

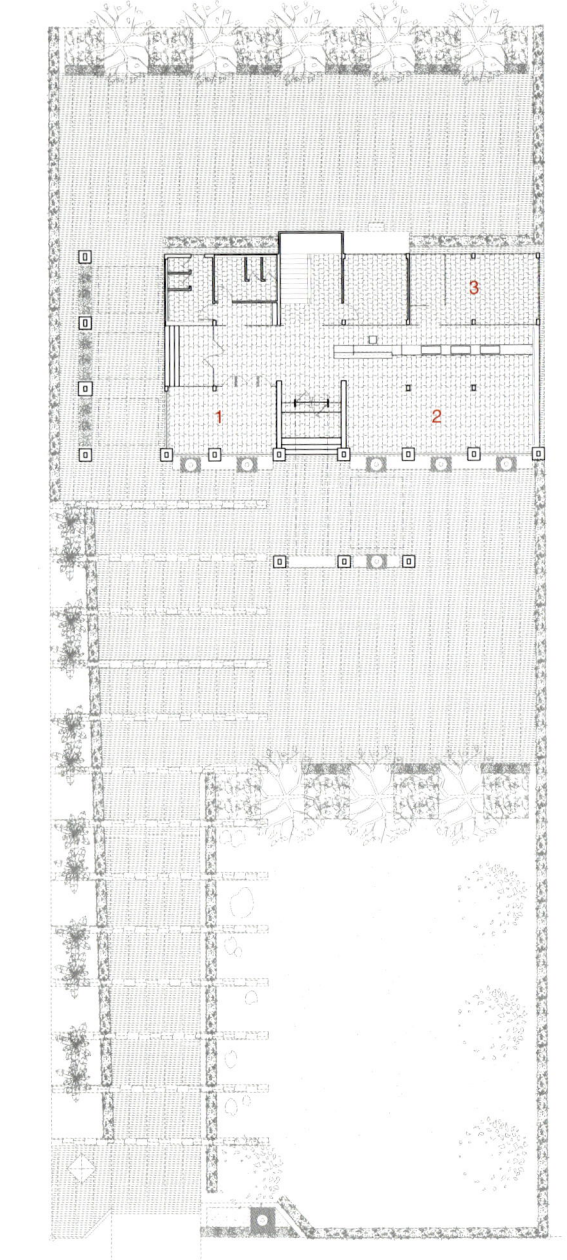

1. Meeting room
2. Lobby
3. Customer service

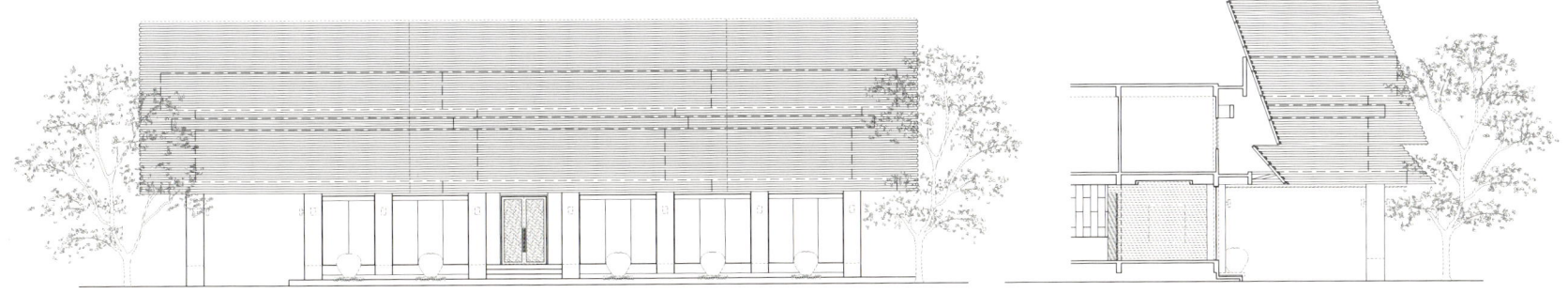

The entrance is pronounced with timber door of a lattice pattern, its 'heveness' aesthetically contrasted with the glass infill on both its sides.

028

Community Organization Development Institute (CODI)

Ashram of Community and Environmental Architect, Arsom Silp Institute of the Arts and Development / Plan Architect

Location :
Navamindra Road, Bangkok

Client :
Community Organization Development Institute (CODI)

Area :
12,975 sq.m.

Year :
2007

Community Organization Development Institute (CODI) is a public organization whose mission is to support and strengthen urban and rural community organizations' housing, social and economic development. The principal design intention was to create a simple architecture that modestly represents the image of CODI as a public organization; friendly and approachable, and to encourage the sense of personal participation and ownership.

The building should also thoroughly reflect the organization's core culture; to work together with the community in partnership and equality, emphasizing horizontal organization, team work and consistent communication, with firm commitment to developing a learning organization.

To offer a welcoming atmosphere for all community organizations and networks, a large plaza was located in front of the main building leading to reception area at ground level. The wide open multi-purpose space is ideal for events and social activities. Further from the reception space, the central open court symbolically defines the heart of community. Users gather and meet before departing to their destinations. Informal meeting places for group discussion and social activities among various users were also located on every floor, connecting to main staircases in order to promote CODI's group learning culture.

Simple, urban architectural elements, such as through-open ground floor, lean-to roof, narrow top-hung windows, as well as random-pattern artificial wood planks, were intentionally used to replicate the characteristic of city housing and create comfortable setting for CODI's clientele. The light feeling created by long-cantilevered roof, wooden wall, free-standing column and through-open ground floor, was a simple architectural language that reflects the oriental sense of the building.

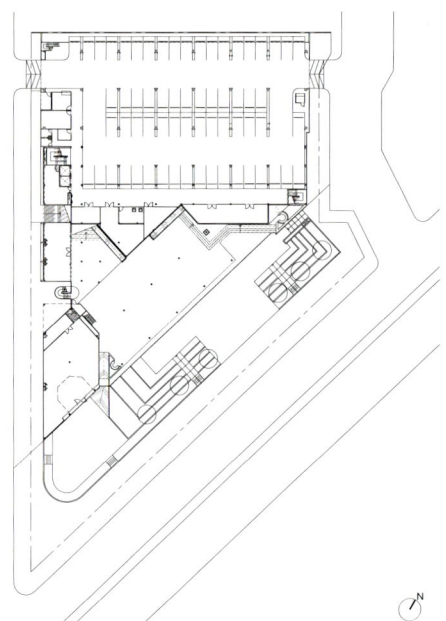

Random-pattern artificial wood plank were used to replicate the character of urban poor housing.

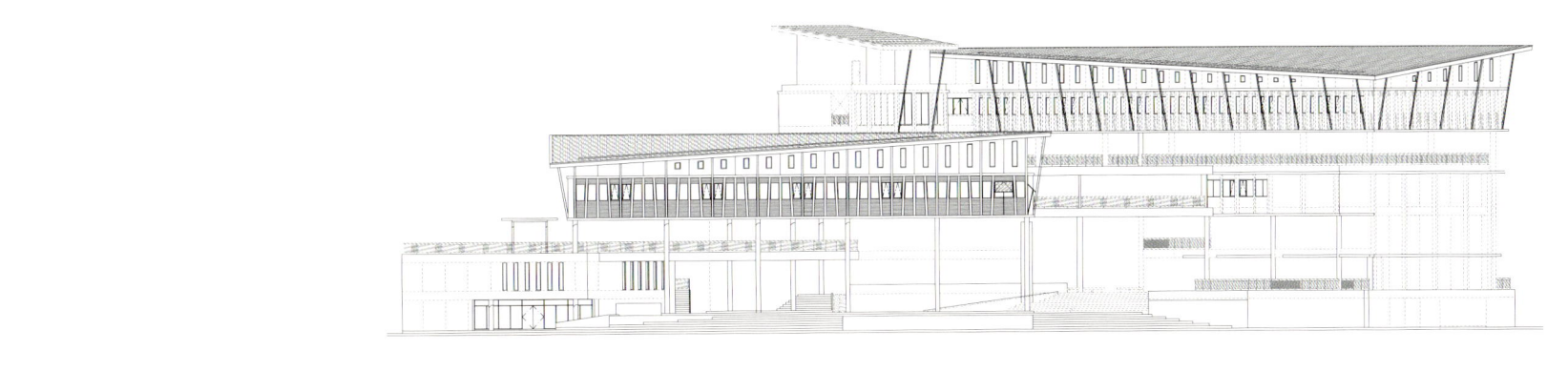

Narrow top-hung window: familaiar element to the urban poor.

The feeling of lightness and transparency are achieved by long-cantileved roof, wooden wall, free-standing column and through-open floor planning.

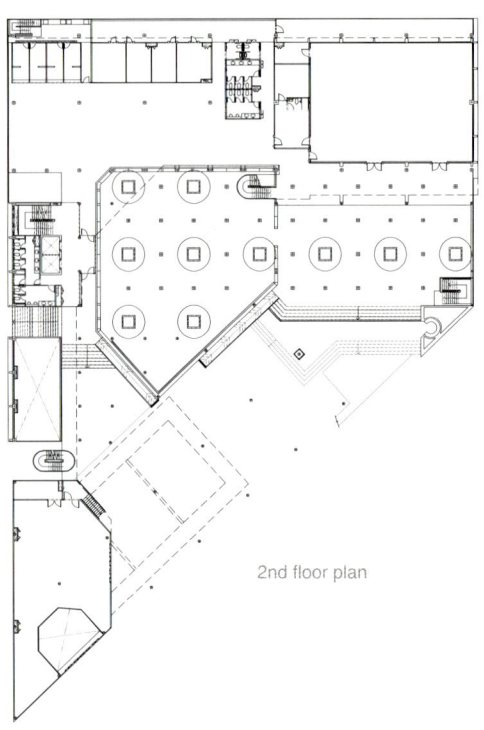

2nd floor plan

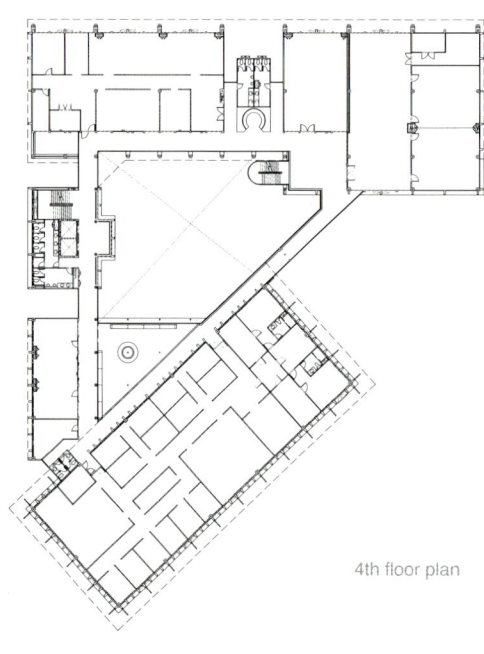

4th floor plan

'*Jai Baan*' - the central open court

029

Stepwise Group Headquarter   ARJ Studio

Location :
Bang Yai, Nonthaburi

Client : Stepwise

Area : 1,800 sq.m.

Year : 2005-2006

Located in the western Bangkok residential neighborhood, Nonthaburi, a small engineering and construction company headquarters consists of a consolidated four-story administration building and storage warehouse.

Responding to the site conditions, intimate setting and a relatively small 1,400 square-meter office space, the building's design balances residential constraints with its infrastructural requirements.

The overall scheme is subtly infused with rectangular shapes for the offices and stair hallways and cylindrical figures for meeting rooms to arrange discrete spaces into their functional uses.

Conceptually, a building's facade depends on a series of delicately tessellated layers. The primary consideration is the combination of tinted glass, corduroyed metal sheets, wooden grills and bare-finished concrete walls on all elevations.

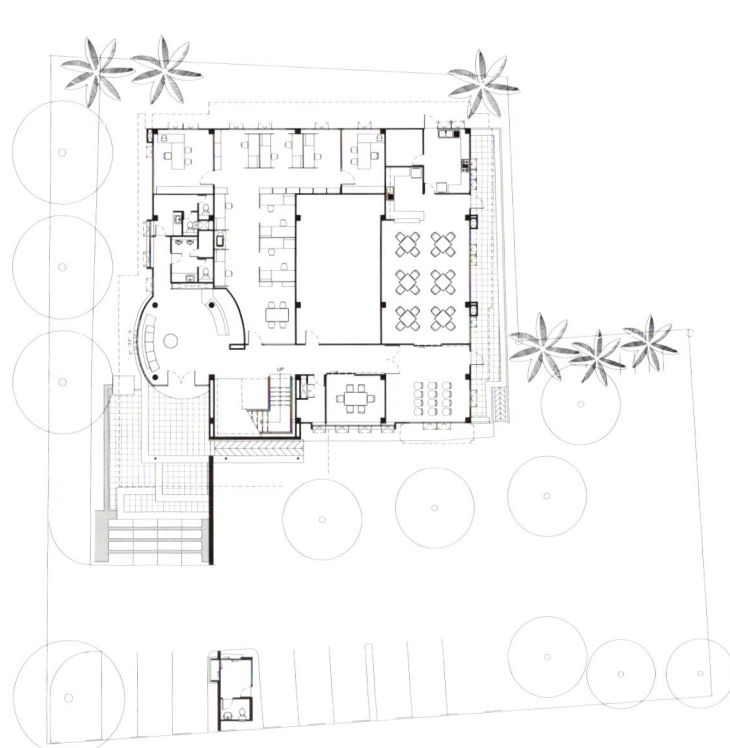

N

The enclose space of stair lobby along 4-5 storey.

Overhange terrace filtering a natural light into working space.

030

Osotspa Building 3 Deca Atelier

Location :
Ram Khamhaeng Road, Bangkok

Client : Osotspa

Area : 10,000 sq.m.

Year : 2005-2007

Scale is the source of meaning and value in architecture. Human scale reflects upon man and his relationship to objects around him. Occasionally, small inspiration can generate massive impact. While walking through the warehouse, the architect noticed the interesting pattern that was created by the unorganized boxes. The voids between the boxes—'in-between spaces'—became a source of inspiration, leading to the design concept of expanding small-scale objects into massive architecture forms.

Each box represents each department's function, and each function affected the pattern of each working unit. Boxes were systematically rearranged (in both vertical and horizontal axes) and shifted to create various interior spaces. What resulted were voids that were directly linked to the building's mass, each with its own unique spatial quality.

The massive center spaces (also caused by the shifting of the architectural boxes) form the main entrance hall. The main approach is through a corridor. Free-form furniture in the waiting area serves as a formal contrast to the geometry of the space and visually weaves together the entire area. Offices are sized according to functional needs, with adjacent support spaces such as meeting and presentation rooms. Concrete, metal, and glass form various volumes, each with varying degrees of transparency and opacity depending on each space's function.

Graphic and signage design were derived from Osotspa's unique corporate identity and by finding a strong, visual vocabulary for each individual department. The industrial character of the warehouse shaped its graphic language, as did the accounting department's use of numbers, which was developed into its graphic identity.

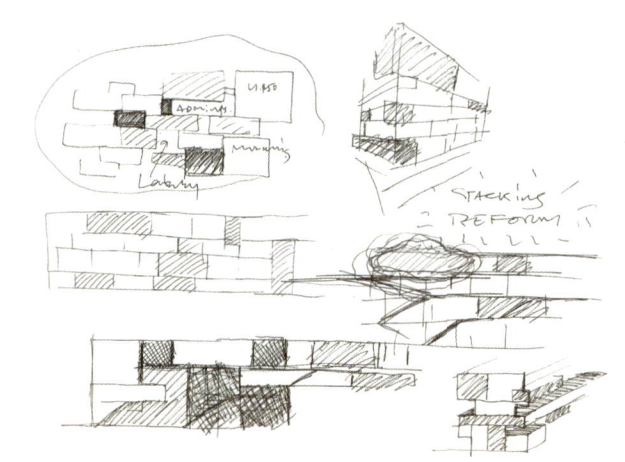

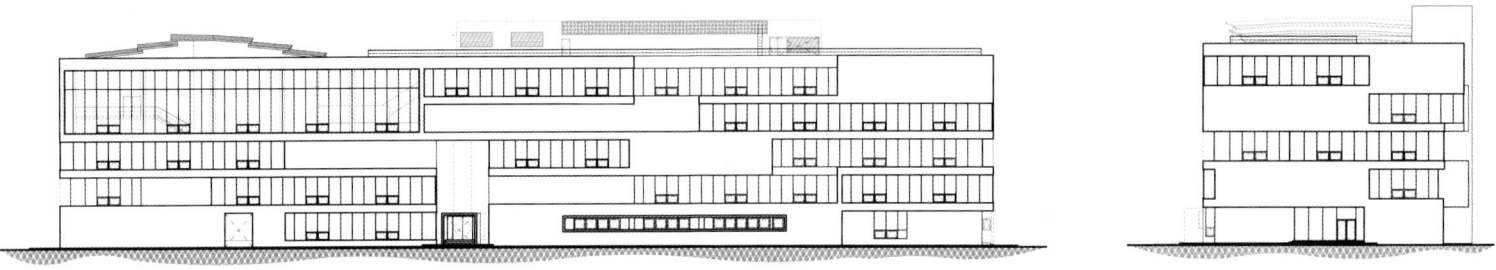

031

Osotspa Canteen   Deca Atelier

Location :
Ram Khamhaeng Road, Bangkok

Client :
Osotspa

Area :
1,500 sq.m.

Year :
2007-2009

Following the conversion of a 50 year old gymnasium into new modern office spaces for Osotspa Co. Ltd. was the design for a new parking structure and a major 10,000 sq. m office building at the company's site.

The immediate task was to create a courtyard canteen in the central space between the building groups. The space was originally used as a parking area and the addition of a new two-story building retains that function below. An inspirational butterfly roof covers the expansive canteen area, creating a dynamic and exciting space underneath. The urban context benefits from the new building through the inclusion of a green roof. This brings an enhanced sense of the courtyard to the occupants of the adjacent buildings. The green roof surface is strategically broken by geometric blocks of air-conditioned compressors obscured by aluminum grills and is punctured with randomly placed skylights which bring light all the way down to the ground floor parking. These details create the sense of a perforated green canopy.

A diagrammatic tree pattern wraps the facade of the second floor. This random and layered pattern emphasizes the natural qualities of the green roof and creates shade and shadow effects throughout the day and conversely during the night.

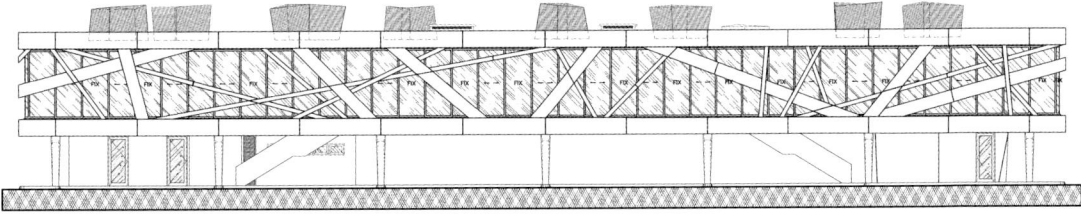

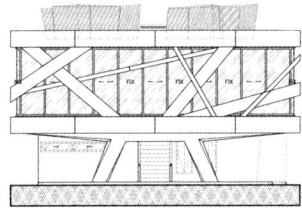

The geometric block of condensing unit obscured by aluminum grills

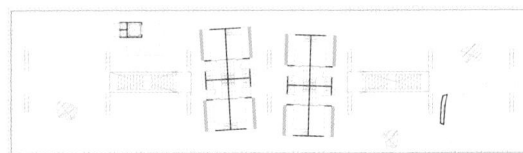

2nd floor plan

Roof plan

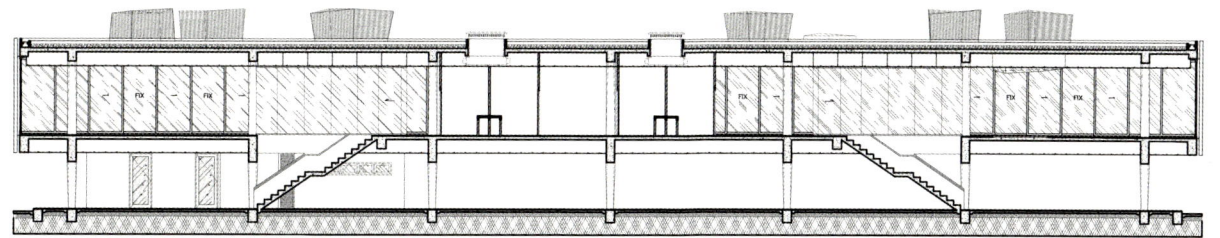

032

SUN ONE

Department of ARCHITECTURE

Location :
Lat Phrao Road, Chatuchak, Bangkok

Client :
Sun Systems Corporation

Area :
1,200 sq.m.

Year :
2007-2009

Located within a low-rise residential neighborhood, software developer SUN ONE's new headquarters challenged designers to balance existing residents' living quality with the new comer's working conditions. A horizontal screening pattern was introduced to the project to preserve the area's serenity; respect residential privacy while simultaneously creating a pleasing working environment for staff. Not only does the screening produce a visual interior/exterior barrier, but it serves as filter generating quality indoor lighting.

The interior was designed to promote a flexible and transparent work environment. In contrast to traditional office space, SUN ONE provides a range of work settings, including bench desks equipped with task lights for concentrated work and informal lounge/bar settings for group meetings and chats. These socially-oriented spaces are intended to promote staff personal interaction over electronic communication.

The most delightful feature of the interior space is the screen design scattered throughout. While the exterior screen design reflects the technological character of company's industry; the interior screen design directly reflects an adventurous owner and staff personality. Industrial material, like colorful PVC strip curtain, has been incorporated throughout the building to reflect the energy and liveliness of these extreme-sport lovers. Besides functioning as space divider and enclosure, the screen serves as the area's privacy level indicator.

With a deliberate architectural strategy, office and home typologies can be perfectly fused into one environment regardless of their architectural style. By creating an understated corporate work space, SUN ONE successfully provides a place that encourages staff collaboration and relaxation.

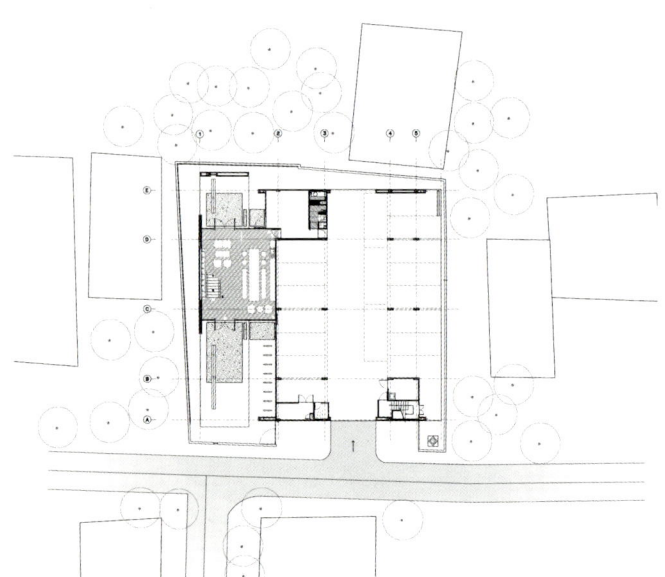

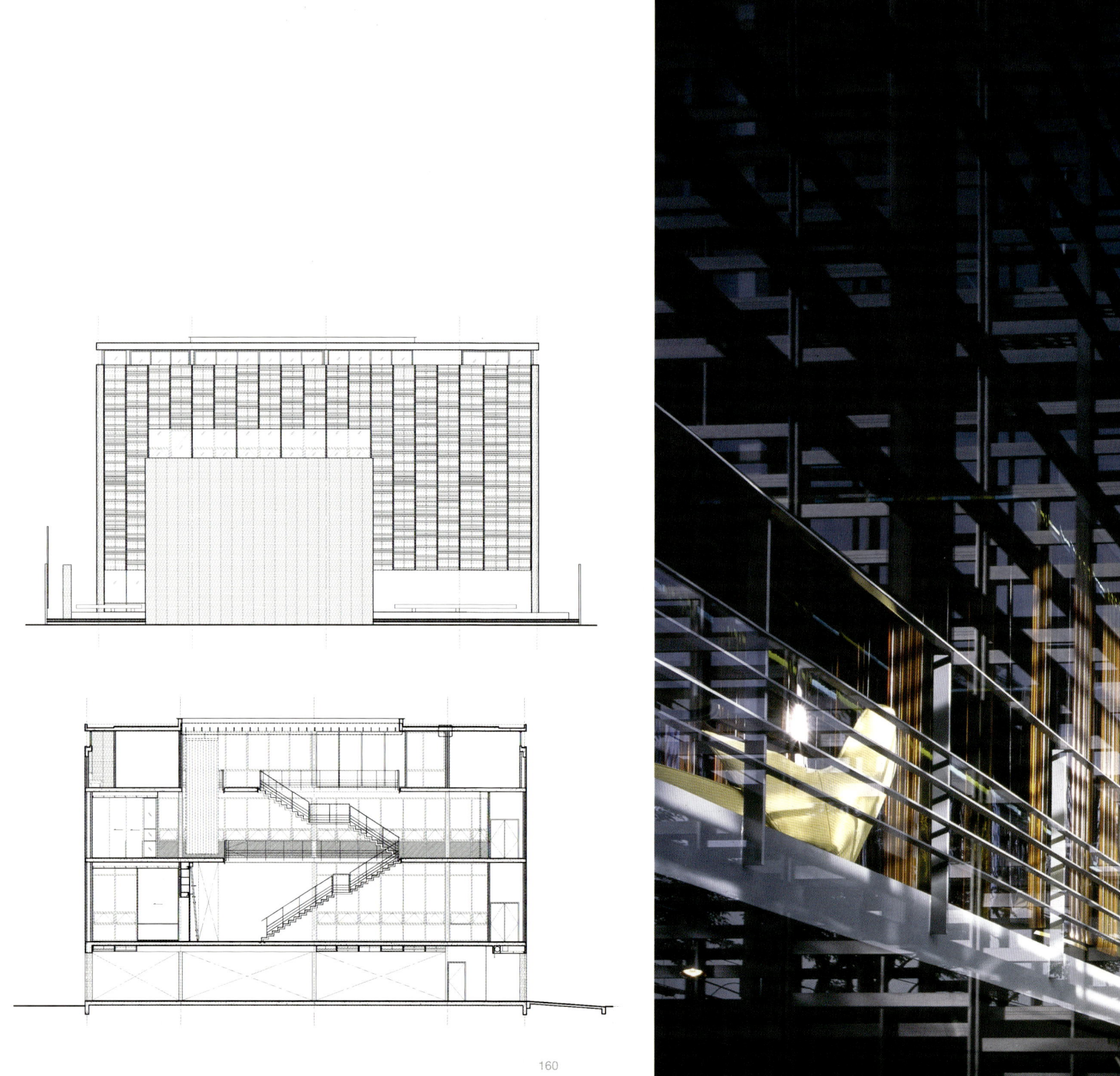

033

Sala @ Sathorn HASSELL

Location : Sathon Road, Bangkok

Client : St Louise

Area : 29,027 sq.m.

Year : 2006-2009

The key architectural requirements were to maximize the western scenic vistas of Bangkok and the Chao Phraya River, while offsetting the impact of solar load and glare after midday.

The tower structure was deliberately orientated to address the approach and take advantage of the major views. Early studies on internal functional use resulted in the selection of the side-core concept to maximize the potential tenantable areas.

The solution was a double screen along the main western facade to filter the solar gain during the peak afternoon periods, and lower the heat gain within the building. This double screen facade incorporating an external ceramic coating has become its unique architectural statement. The concept also identified lower overall loads on the A/C plant required to cool individual floors.

The northern street facade is treated with a glazed curtain wall system enabling visual access to the energetic views. Strategically placed decorative vertical aluminium blades located on the curtain wall provide shade across this glazed wall during winter when the sun is at its lowest elevations.

Similarly along the southern façade, in direct response to the early morning solar sun-path, the external aluminium sunshades are located horizontally to align with the building fabric.

Finally, the east facade consists of a structural sheer wall wrapped with a random pattern of composite cladding. Strategically located vertical openings in the external lift walls frame the dynamic movement of the passenger lifts.

The design implements key sustainability elements that responsibly responded to site, solar load and climate.

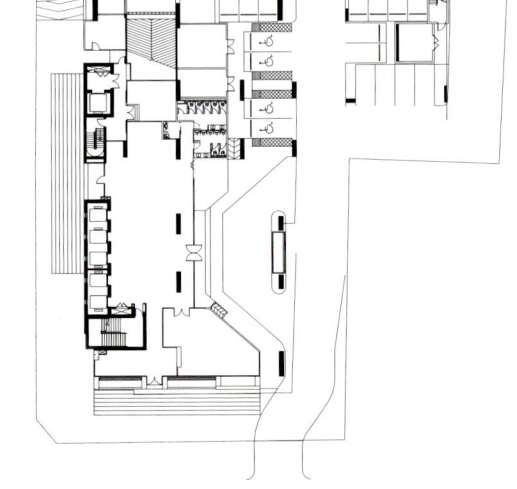

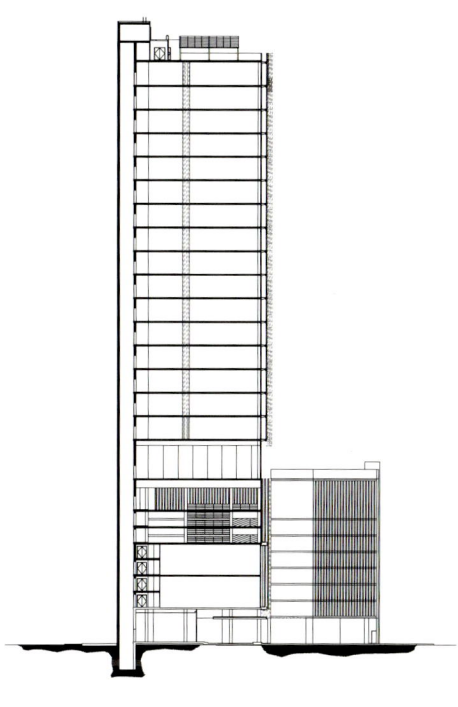

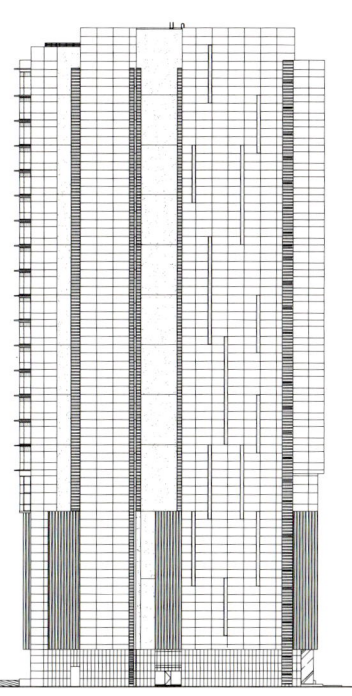

Main entrance feature wall

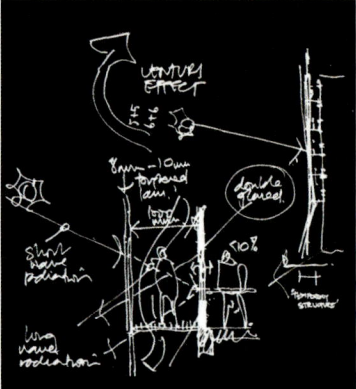

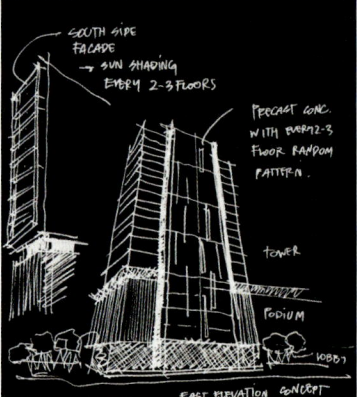

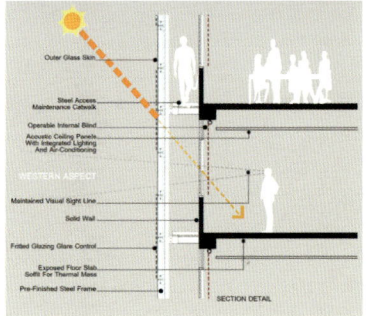

Double skin concept

034

Phuket Gateway

IDIN Architects

Location :
Thepkrasatthree Road, Phuket

Client :
Phuket Provincial Administrative Organization

Area :
1,600 sq.m.

Year :
2005-2007

This scenic town is a melting pot of cultures and races represented by diverse local, Chinese, Muslim and Sino-Portuguese architectural styles. However, the project does not reveal any single culture significantly, but interprets these local forms in combination with native materials to create a contemporary pattern and function.

The project, developed as a public space is comprised of a contemporary building and landscape. The building is linearly positioned facing the province entrance, utilizing the original site contour. The landmark exhibits a striking example of Phuket's historical 'lively sculpture motif.

The sculptures include a 100-meter colonnade of concrete columns announcing the entrance to the Sino-Portuguese styled building. A covered passage connects each edifice. A high sculptured-granite column pays homage to tin as the local natural resource that brought wealth to the community years ago. Each piece of granite represents a disparate culture that blended into the unique town of Phuket. The granite column still acts as a lighthouse for this prominent destination.

Functional space is hidden behind the colonnade sculpture and trees. A service area comprised of a tourist information center, government office, police station, restaurant, auditorium and Islamic prayer space is designed as a pavilion area; divided by pocket sized parks, where natural light seeps through the translucent roof.

Texture of high column sculture

N

Viewing point area and colonnade scultures.

Colonnade sculpture

035

PM Center Office Building

Ongsa Architects

Location :
Khlong Kum, Bueng Kum, Bangkok

Client :
Presentation Media Supply

Area :
4,600 sq.m.

Year :
2002

The PM Center is a combination office, warehouse and sculpture gallery. The primary intention is to explore a relationship between building function; its forms, users and site, a rather narrow and long proportion. The key notion of the architectural strategy is to exploit the complexity and contradiction of these functions.

Design principle is provocative, activated by "juxtapositing intervention" of horizontal lines and rectangular masses composed into a simple lay-out of rooms and functions. These simplistic modules of rectangular masses are placed with emphasis on negative volume of the space in between and the exploration of the interrelationship between indoor and outdoor spaces.

The architectural composition of the building was developed to express the three main programmatic functions: office, warehouse, and sculpture gallery. Each of these functions is distinctly articulated in the building massing. The volumes are interrelated, bringing into life the volumetric unit between boxes and allowing for light and nature to invade. The three functions were arranged to form a central sculptural court that unifies the entire project. The court was and bordered on three sides by building elements facing inward. Thus, it is the key element to establish a powerful sense of place that leads to the Sculpture Center beyond.

The complex is characterized by a strong horizontal line of building masses, in contrast to the warehouse's bulky mass. The office masses were raised above ground level, occupying the upper area of the building complex. The masses were slightly skewed to dramatize an impression of lightness and at the same time served as a sign of entry and shelter for visitors.

Sculpture courtyard

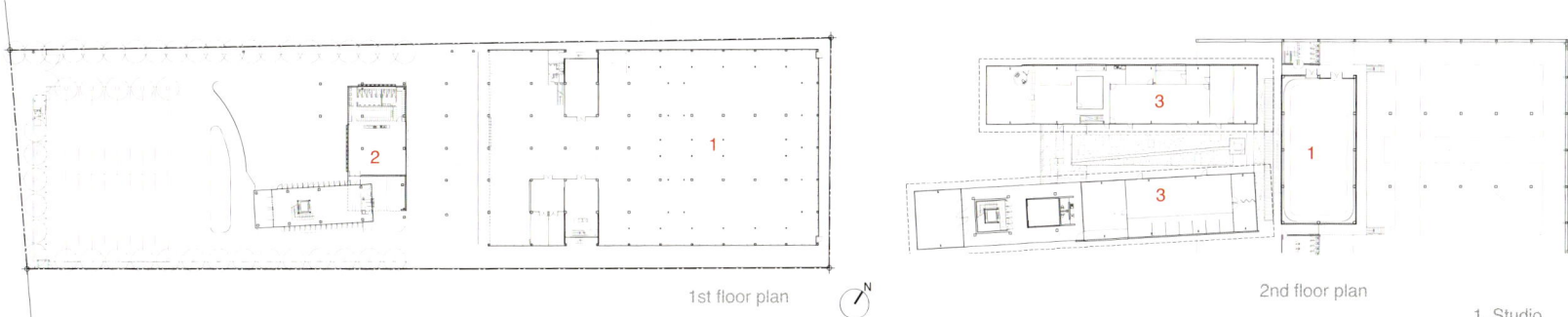

1st floor plan

N

2nd floor plan

1. Studio
2. Canteen
3. Office

Visitor circulation core

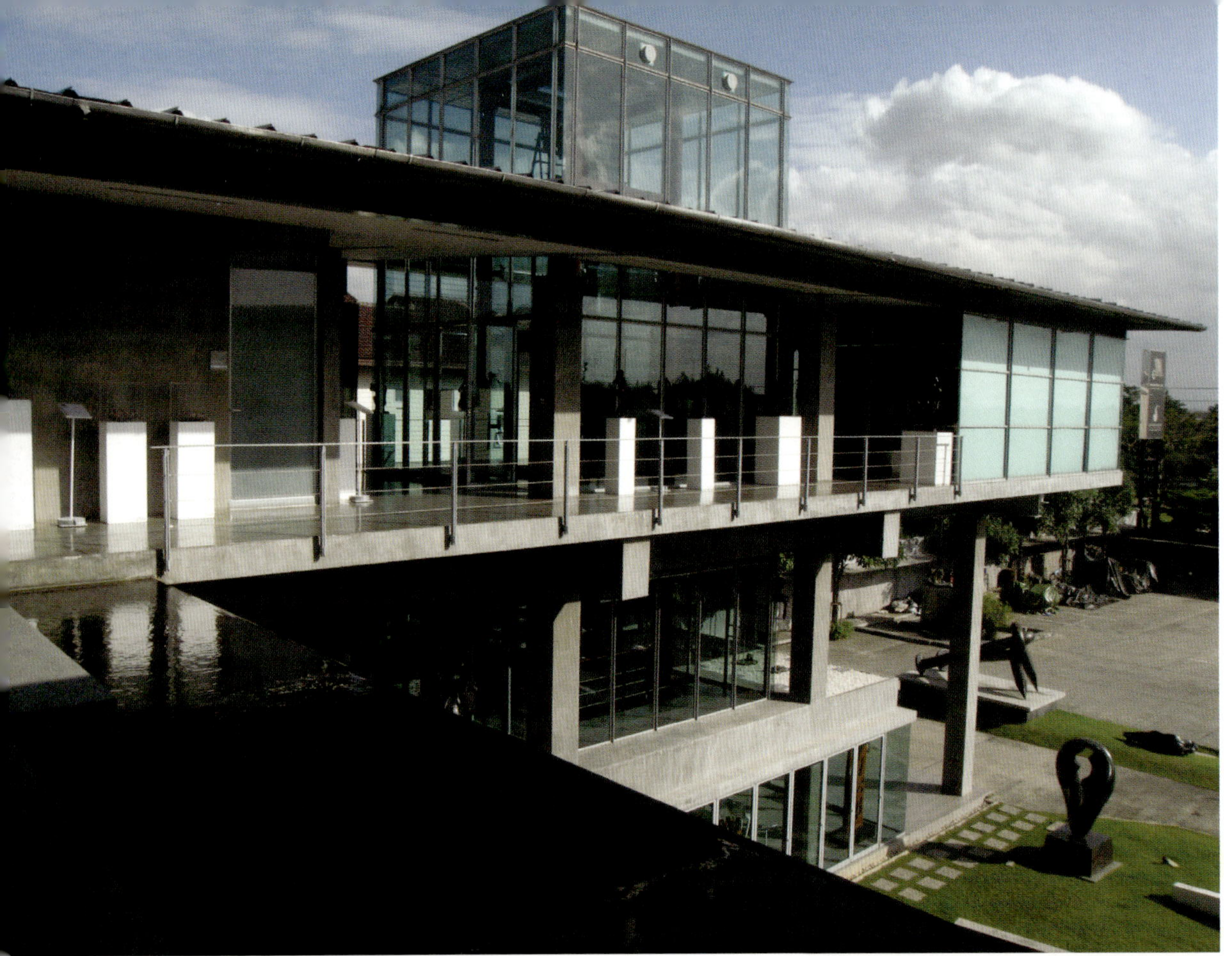

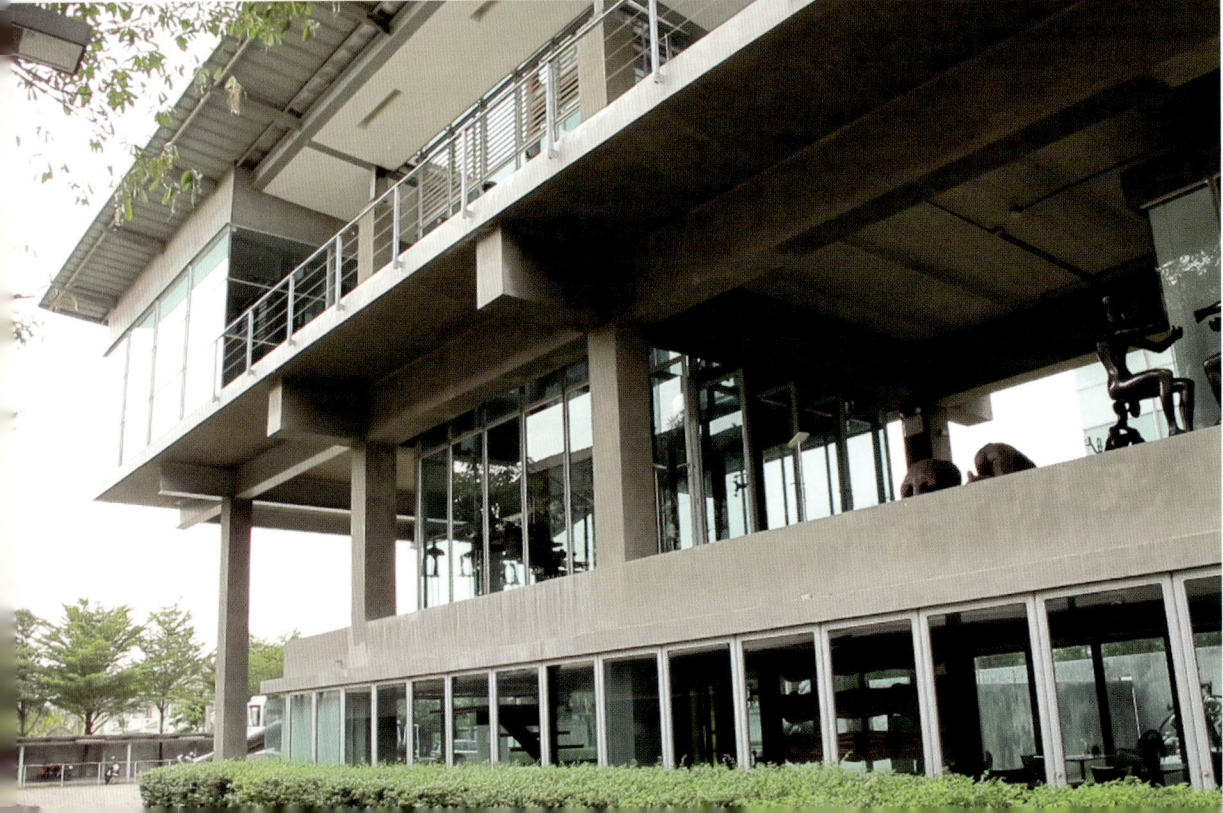

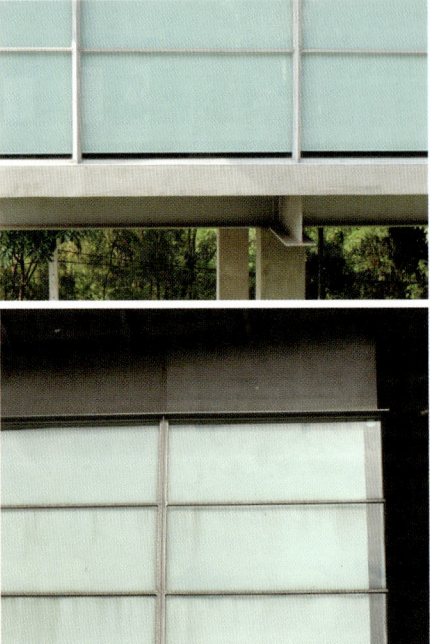

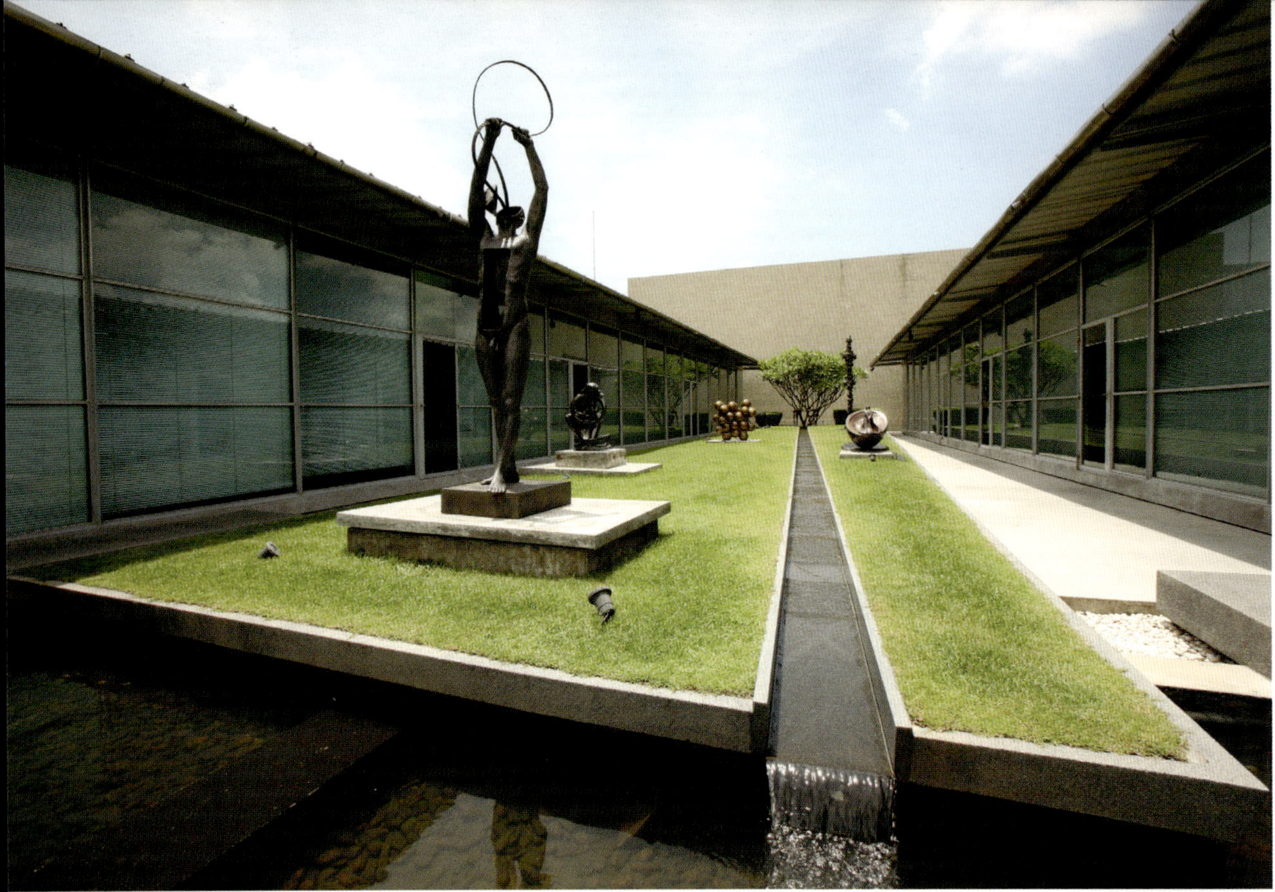

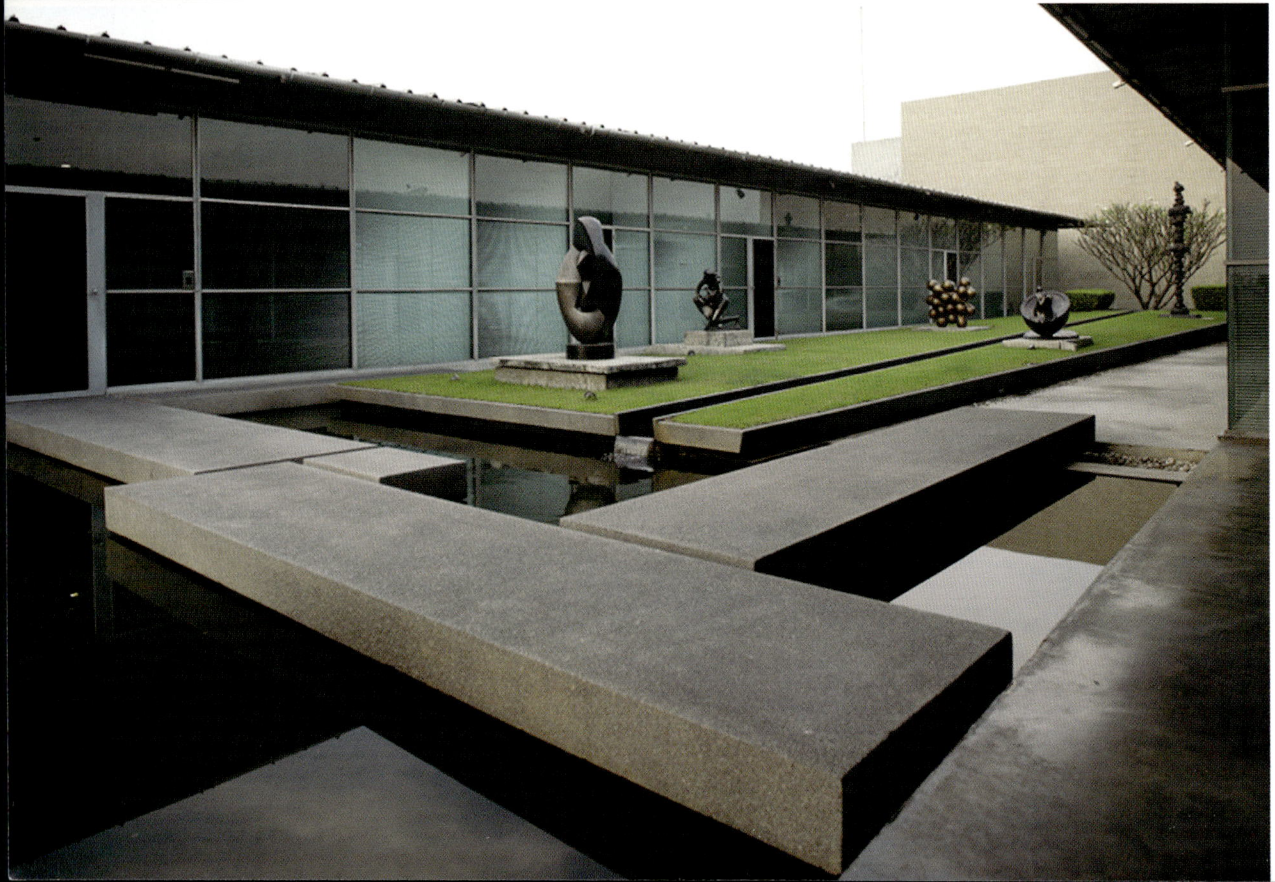

Sculpture courtyard

Museum

036

Bank of Thailand Headquarter
Plan Associates / Plan Architect / Tandem Architect

Location :
Samsen Road, Bangkok

Client :
Bank of Thailand

Area :
86,000 sq.m.

Year :
2002–2007

It is essential to understand the Bank of Thailand headquarters' expansion site and its surrounding historical context before appreciating this project. The site was surrounded by several historical buildings such as the Bangkhunprom Palace and Devavesm Palace. Although it was a new construct, the Thai National Bank expansion architecture was designed with respect to its historical surroundings and was blended into the historical context of the site.

Samsen Road, the main access point to the expansion, was extended for the new building. A new visual axis was created, which influenced the building's positioning. The new visual axis was also expressed by the opening plaza which was used as the main entry to the building.

The headquarters plan required a complicated layer of functionality. Security and functional usage were two of the key issues for the design planning of the new bank. Building zoning was arranged according to its function and usage. The main office was connected to the existing building, while the service and meeting areas were placed next to the office for convenience use.

The Bank of Thailand architecture is contemporary, but humble to its surroundings. The use of natural light during the day is incorporated into the design for sustainable energy savings. This project was awarded an Association of Siamese Architect (ASA) 2009 Green Award.

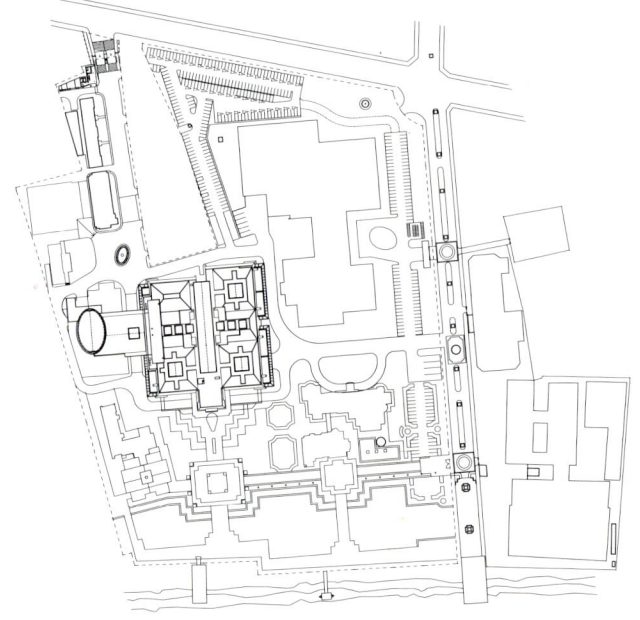

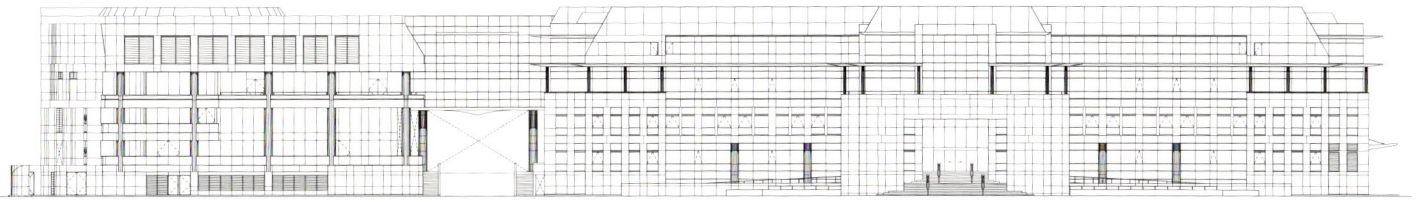

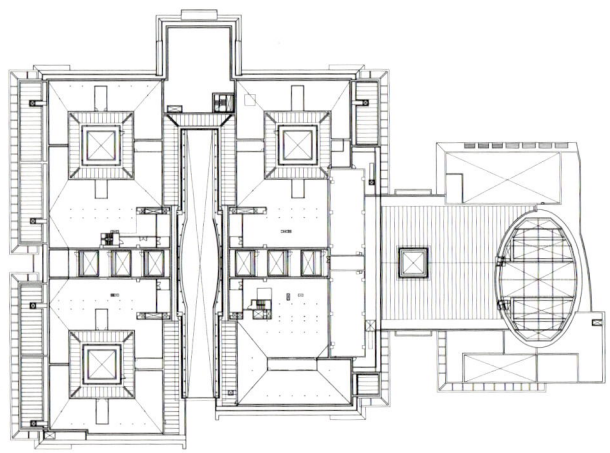

Entrance passage way

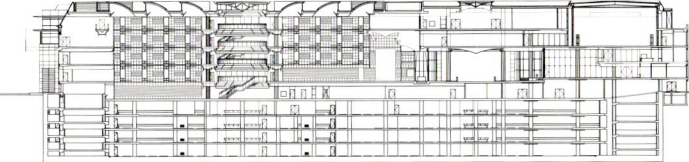

Light well details

The Office Plus Plankrich

Location :
Suthep, Muang, Chiang Mai

Client :
Taipong Wongkasem-Yannawut

Area :
3,694 sq.m.

Year :
2008-2009

Renovation in design is this project's mantra. The old former warehouse is converted into a modern, fully-functional office space. This 2-story building is renovated by keeping its structure and roof with the new office design.

The new plan combines the steel-concrete structure with a brand new front facade design, resulting in an original overall exterior character. The new facade is parallel with main access road. The reception lobby welcomes a flood of natural light and continues through the main court, functioning as an access path to each office space in the outdoor terrace.

This main central court will also generates ventilating breezes, bringing both fresh air and natural light through the building's inner space

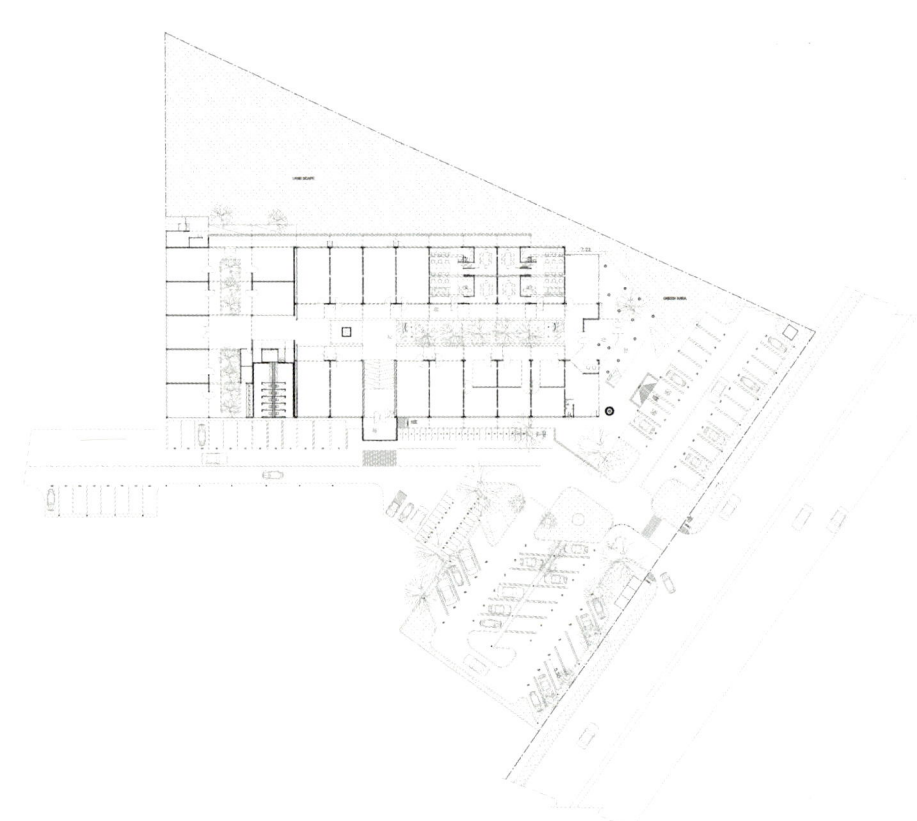

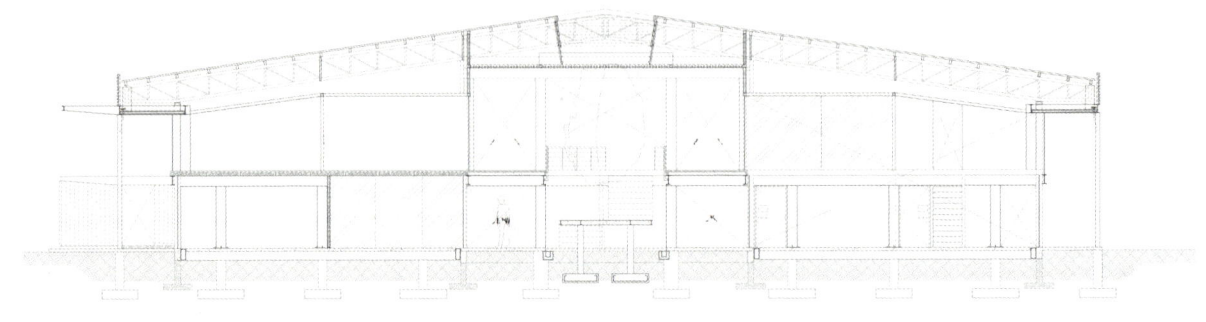

038

Q. House Lumpini Park

Robert G. Boughey and Associates

Location :
South Sathon Road, Sathon, Bangkok

Client :
Quality Houses

Area :
120,000 sq.m.

Year :
1994-2006

Q House is located at the intersection of Wireless, Sathorn, and Rama IV Roads, creating a significant urban element on one of Bangkok's most prominent crossroads.

The 38-story complex is divided into 3 main zones; the office tower, a public Plaza, and a low rise building which houses restaurants, health and commercial activities. The building form takes advantage of the site's exposure and location. In order to emphasis the plaza and to create a unique building form, the Tower is tapered on two sides. This taper also pays homage to traditional Thai architecture, with the walls slightly off perpendicular. The golden roof shapes, influenced by Thai motifs and forms, reflect light both night and day and identify the complex from near and afar. A large grid imposed on the facade adds scale and color to the monochrome glass.

The two different zones of the building are expressed on the exterior with the gold grid being the dominant element unifying both major edifice elements. The lower roof, which sits on a circular platform, reflects in smaller scale the main Tower roof.

Lofty public spaces on the ground floor allow visual access from the plaza. The main plaza is kept vehicle free. Access is from the South side of the building with direct connection to the main lobby.

The main materials are concrete structure, glass curtain wall and gold colored aluminum tower pinnacles and accents.

The roof shapes identify the complex from near and far.

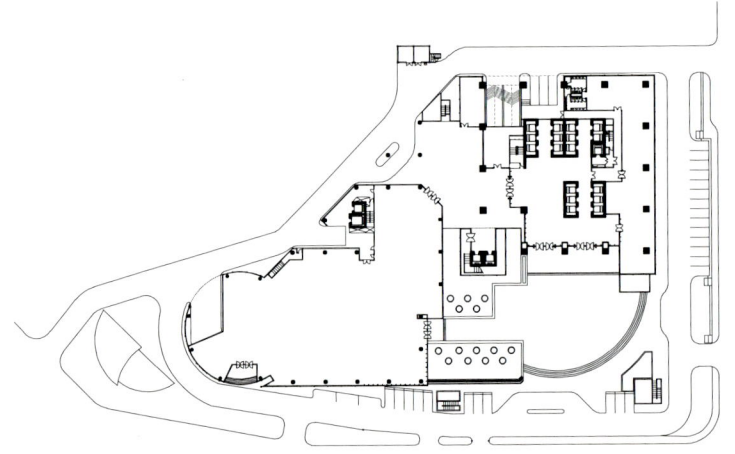

N

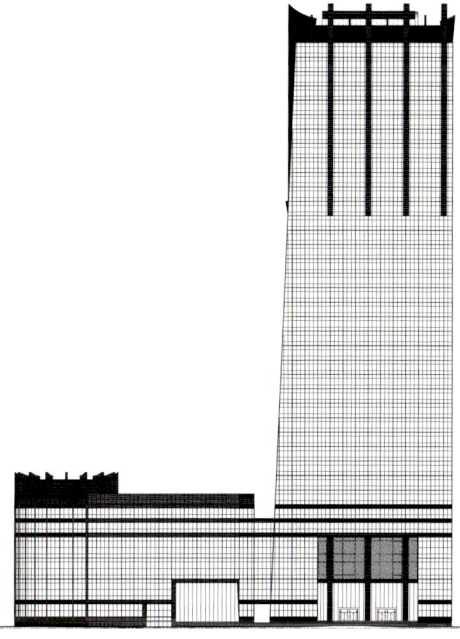

Main lobby & elevator hall

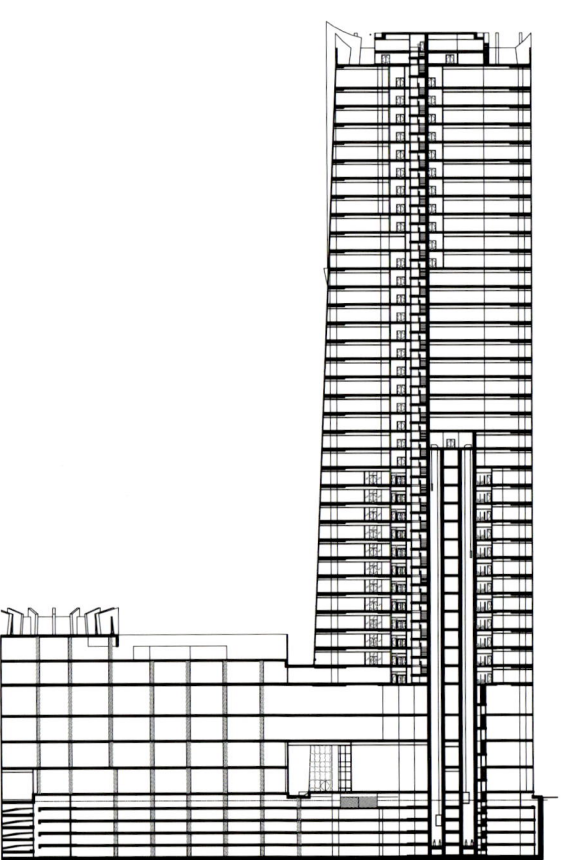

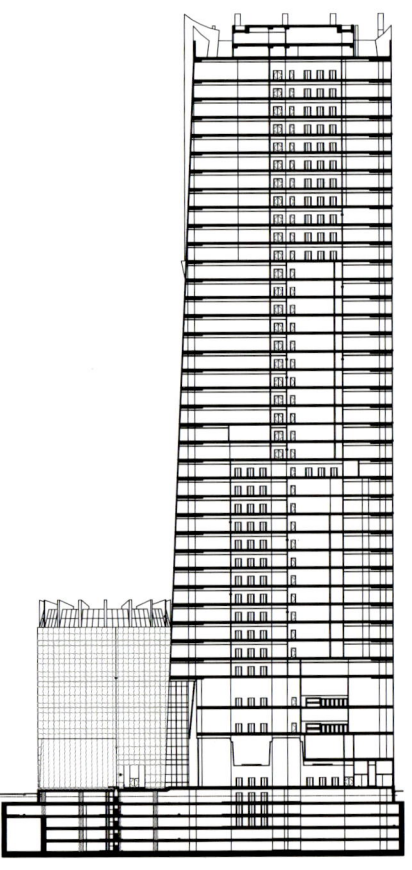

039

SCG Experience   Architects 49

Location :
At Narong-Ramindra Road, Bangkok

Client :
SCG Experience

Area :
6,200 sq.m.

Year :
2007- 2009

Originally a winning proposal from the 'Cement Thai Building Products Gallery' design competition", the idea was moved from the construction site and housed in the Project CDC or Crystal Design Center. The center collects all types of building construction and design products. Located at the front access point of an 11.2 Hectares campus, the building's 20-meter high glass façade welcomes visitors at a first glance. Not only the nation's first cement producer, Cement Thai is a public company with a long history of continuous expansion; becoming Thailand's largest and most advanced industrial conglomerate. The design takes inspiration from the company's history.

An enormous concrete slab gradually tilts away from the floor slab to become the wall, expands and pierces the sky to become the roof above its starting point. The combined concrete plane forms the 3-story building which holds the exhibition space, the reading area and product expertise consulting service on the first floor and the library, designers club, material library and Cement Thai's product display area on the second. The third floor holds the administrative offices and displays some oversized products.

The building's shape is largely defined by the property boundaries; however, the building's concrete is freed to become its own element. The edge of the slab defines the building's floor shape and the open space by connecting and joining the disparate elements.

Interestingly, all building components were constructed with products from one single company and its affiliated groups.

1. SCG Experience
2. Crystal Design Center

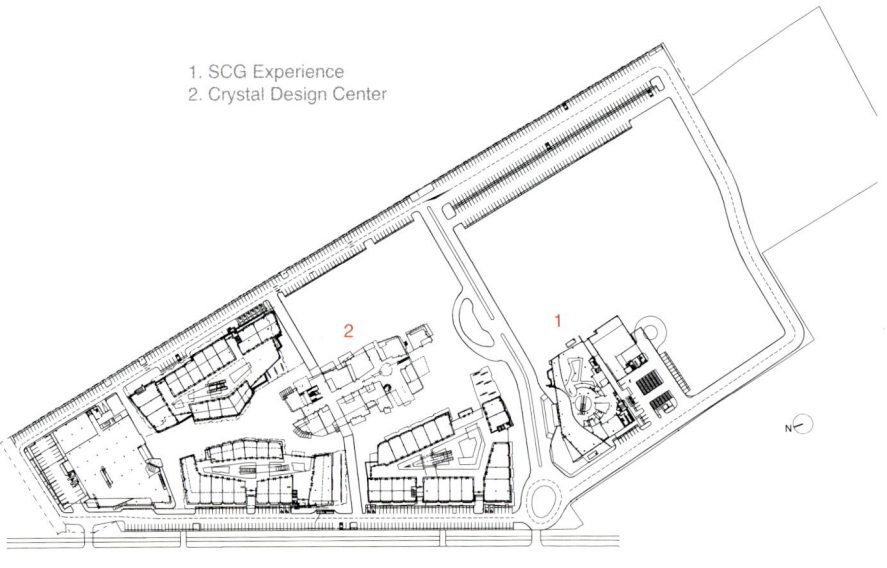

196

Enormous concrete slab reflects the advanced
innovation of the company.

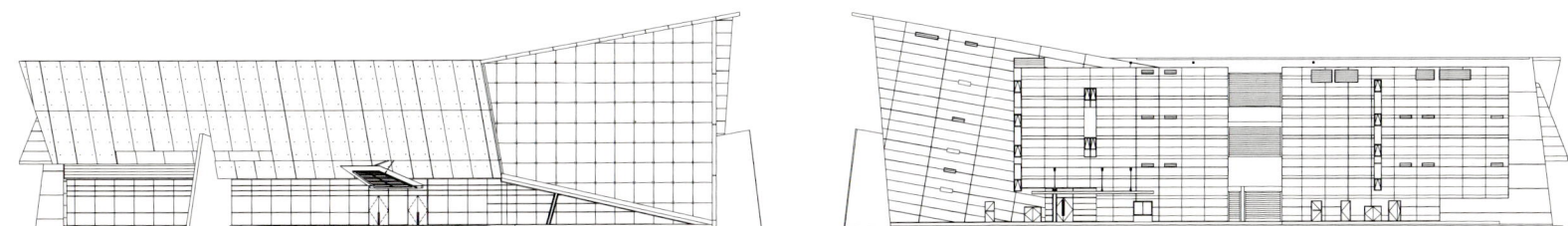

1 2

1. The Atrium
2. Library

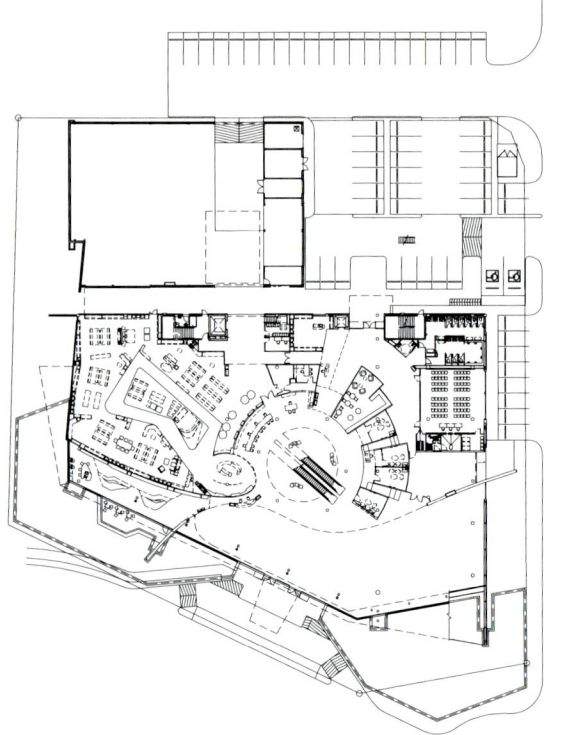
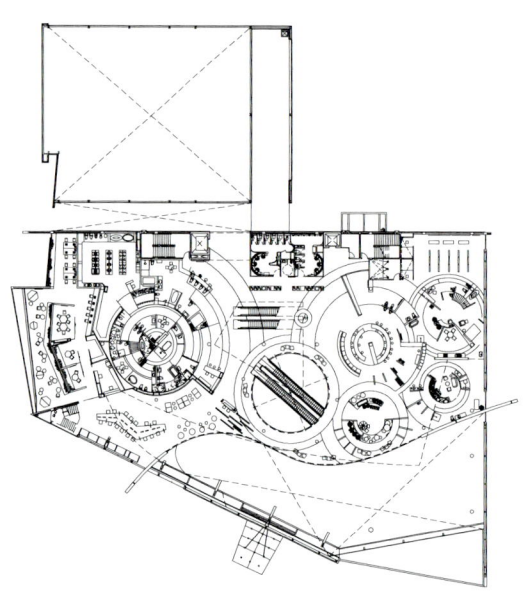
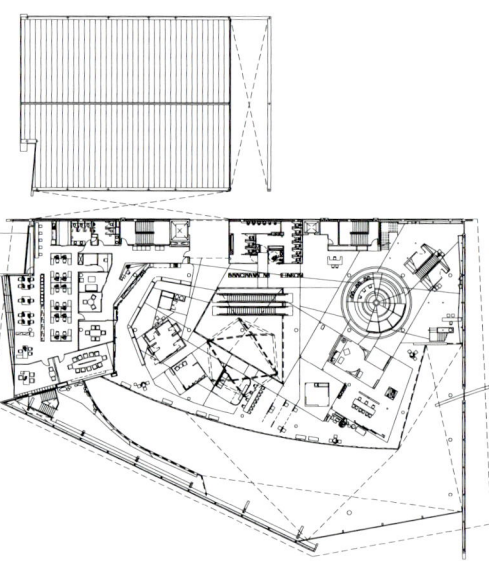

040

The Oriental Fine Art   Composition A

Location :
Had Surin, Bang Toa, Phuket

Client :
Mr. Charoen Sasiluksananukul

Area :
860 sq.m.

Year :
2001-2003

The Oriental Fine Art is a renovation project, developed from a four-story shophouse. The building is located in front of Surin Beach, Phuket, with the Andaman Sea to its west and a mountain to its south. The renovated and extended building was designed to house an antique oriental art gallery on the lower three floors and the owner's residence on the fourth floor.

As the existing building has no historical significance, the design strategy was to modify the whole building, keeping only the building's framework. The design aimed to capitalize on the quality of the surrounding view and to emphasize the rich details of the antique art. A simple form and neutral color, both inside and outside, were chosen to contrast with the richly detailed objects displayed. Natural materials such as stone and wood were chosen for the building's facade to blend with the natural sea and the mountain environment; which at the same time distinguished the project from the surrounding buildings.

The interior spaces were organized as a series of horizontally and vertically linked open wells and solid spaces that are connected to the exterior view through the building's openings.

041

Exhibition Gallery, Chulalongkorn University
Faculty of Architecture, Chulalongkorn University

Location : Chulalongkorn University, Phyathai Road, Bangkok

Client : Chulalongkorn University

Year : 2008-2009

The new exhibition gallery of Chulalongkorn University is a renovation of the previous Chemistry 3 building. It was originally and specifically built as chemistry laboratories and classrooms for the Faculty of Science in 1961. The original building was an L-shaped plan, using the most advanced wide-spanned structure at the time— concrete waffle slab. The original façade showed prefabricated corrugated concrete sunscreen which represented the popular Modern architectural trend in Thailand during 1960s - 1970s.

As a result of the recent university master plan on zoning, Chemistry 3 building is in the North-South axis zone functioning as one of campus main circulation cores. Its location is determined as a node for supporting facilities to nearby faculties. The beneficial wide-spanned structure and its place between Faculties of Architecture and Fine and Applied Arts calls for a university gallery to exhibit student work. In addition its vicinity close to the university historical buildings around the flag pole makes the new gallery a suitable showcase and welcome place for all guests to Chulalongkorn University.

The university master plan suggests a trimming of the western wing of the original L-shaped plan building to open an outdoor space joining the gallery with the adjacent historic Chemistry 1 Building, a masterpiece of Thai early modern architecture in Neoplastic style. The latter building has recently been renovated as the new university photo archives and music library. The deletion of the western wing of the Chemistry 3 Building requires special reinforcement to the remaining structure. A ramp is added to the west as main circulation to the exhibition spaces of each floor while providing elevated view of the outdoor court. Transparency and reflection is the key concept to the new façade design, firstly to give a contemporary modern look to the building. Secondly, the glass facade provides transparency for the passers-by to see what's going on inside the building. Pivoting panels behind the glass facade make possible the flexibility of controlled natural-light for temporary exhibitions inside. At certain angles the glass facade allows transparency through the space within and simultaneously reflecting the surrounding trees outside.

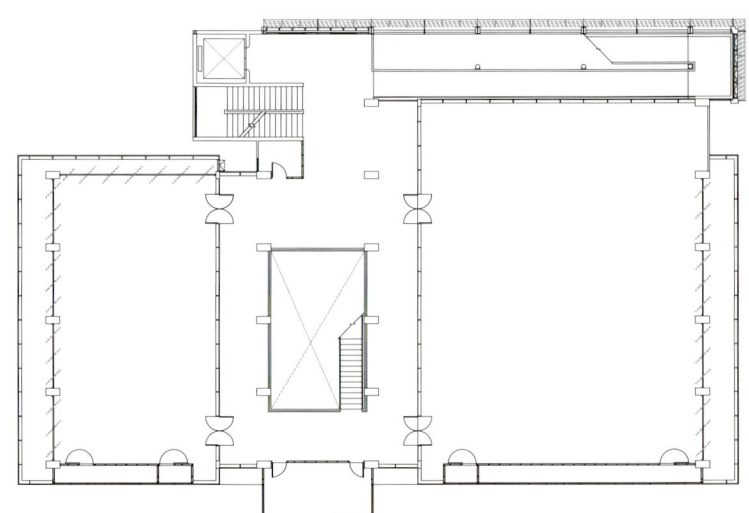

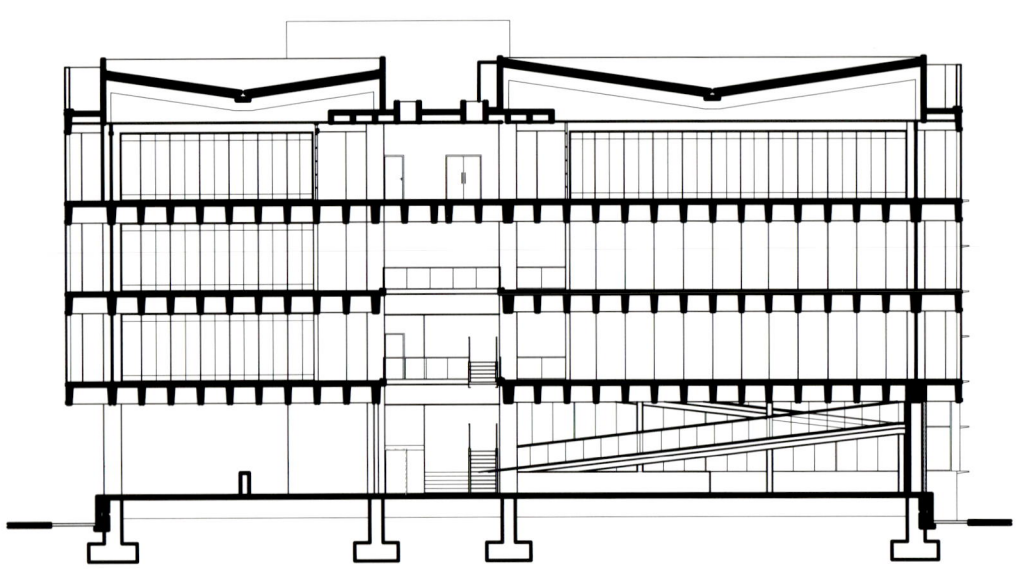

042

The First Royal Factory at Fang the Museum
Interior Architecture 103

Location :
Ban Yang, Chiang Mai

Client :
The Crown Property Bureau

Area :
8,000 sq.m.

Year :
2007-2009

Forty years ago, Ban Yang, Fang District was covered by opium fields and became a starting point of a drug transporting to the global community. It was not until King Bhumipol Aduljadej visited that the drug situation gradually changed. His Majesty encouraged the villagers to replace their fields with other economic crops and also set up a cooperative group.

In 2006, torrential rains caused flashfloods in Fang District. The incident destroyed the Royal Factory. Subsequently, H.R.H. Princess Maha Chakri Sirindhorn initiated to restore the Royal Factory and build a museum aiming to demonstrate publicly how dedicated His Majesty the King was and is to his people.

The natural sincerity design concept was inspired by King Bhumipol Adulyadej's simple 'Think big, do small' adage. The plan follows the unique local architecture by adhering to the villagers' usable and functional space application.

The project consists of main 6 buildings with layouts in harmony with community house patterns. Spaces are practical and functional; raised floors reduce flood damage and open spaces in the buildings' centers and terraces operate as multifunctional activity areas.

Environmentally friendly materials were utilized throughout the plan. Designers selected clay roof tiles and lightweight brick walls to reduce interior heat and included engineering systems that recycled unavoidable water and garbage waste by transforming it into biological gas used internally.

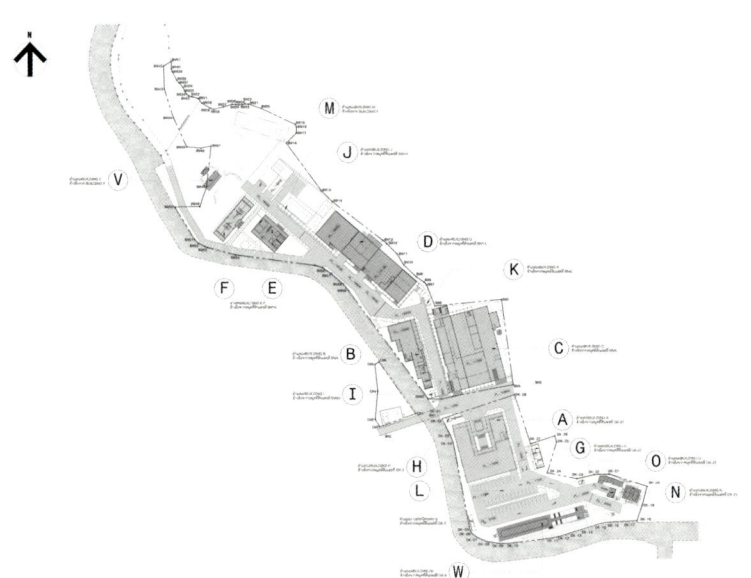

043

Plearnwan OPENBOX

Location :
Hua Hin, Prachuap Khiri Khan

Client :
Phattra Sahawat

Area :
3,770 sq.m.

Year :
2009

The development started with the owner's dream to create a place for lively and colorful activities on family land; it should accommodate a broad variety of activities while it reflects a memorable, unique style. With no other preconceived ideas about the appearance, the owner came with the first concept keyword, 'Ngan Wat' (Temple festival).
The designers addressed key project challenges. With 16.0 m frontage and 148.5 m back property line, the site was both small and odd shaped. The location was on the main road to Hua Hin, but nowhere near the beach. This site was not ideal for developing a place to draw crowds and activities.

The Thai '1950' to 1960's era style was selected for its colorful, enjoyable and romantic design that still had great nostalgic impact today. Finally, the concept evolved from 'Temple Festival' to 'Eco, Retro Village' portrayed as a 'Live museum'.
Master planning began by placing the main open space in the center of the property, completely surrounded by buildings and landscape to contain and intensify feelings and experiences. Building alignment and axis was adjusted to create the illusion of a larger space.

Front building space created a 'gate' or 'time tunnel' effect, taking visitors back to another time and place. The exterior, clad in old and rustic materials, combined with the heavily decorated interior, producing a surreal and photogenic effect. Landform is gradually raised from entrance towards the back to create a lower parking and service floor. Despite differences in levels throughout the development, wheelchair access covers all areas.

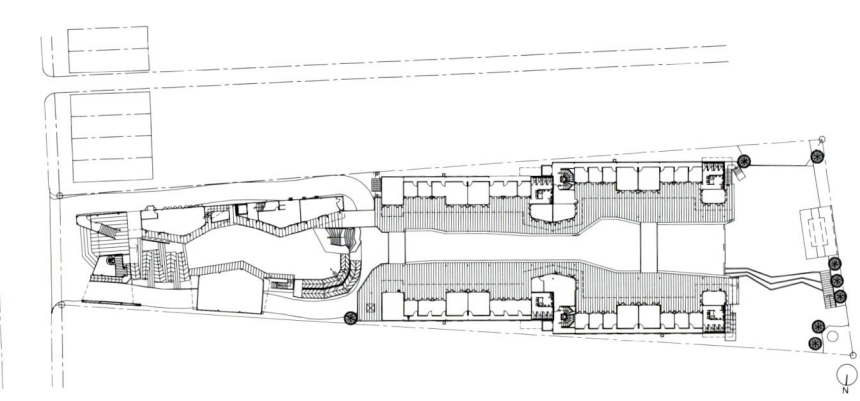

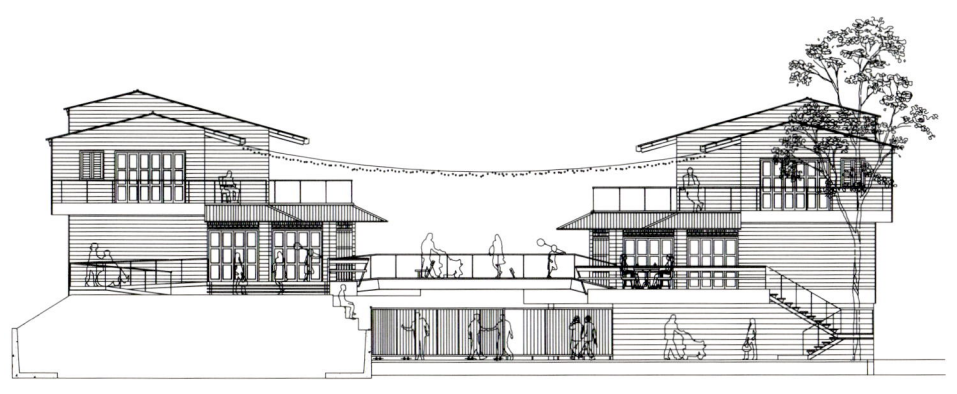

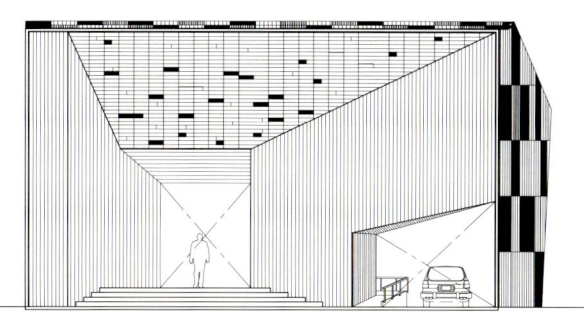

Translucent roof tiles give unique random glows
to the building elevation at night.

1		1
1		

Opposite :

1. Outside facade composed of different types of corrugated
   roof tiles. Some are tilted to provide natural ventitation.

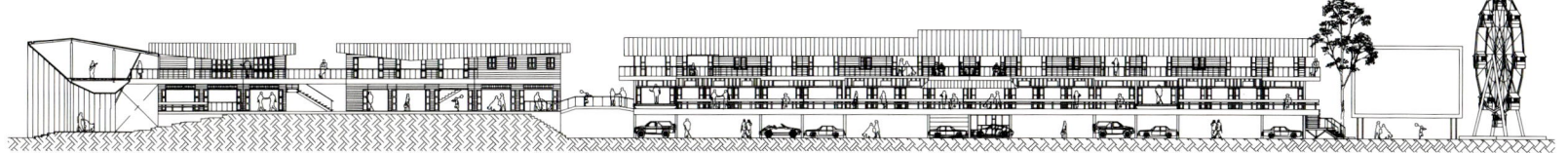

044

Prince of Songkhla University International Convention Center

Plan Associates

Location :
Hat Yai, Songkhla

Client :
Prince of Songkhla University

Area :
17,500 sq.m.

Year :
2004 – 2008

The University of Prince Songklanakarin, Songkla Province's international convention hall is designed as the heart of Southern provinces special event hosting. The convention hall layout was analyzed to find the optimal functional and architectural positioning.

Project planning plays the most significant design role for the hall. As the result, important fundamentals such as the terminal drop-off, traffic flow, structural system and arrangement of usable and service space are taken into the consideration to create a structure of international quality.

The one story building is placed horizontally in order to make it the site focal point. The southern Thai vernacular heavily influences the project, where building esthetics is expressed with proportional as well as symbolic architecture.

Main entrance

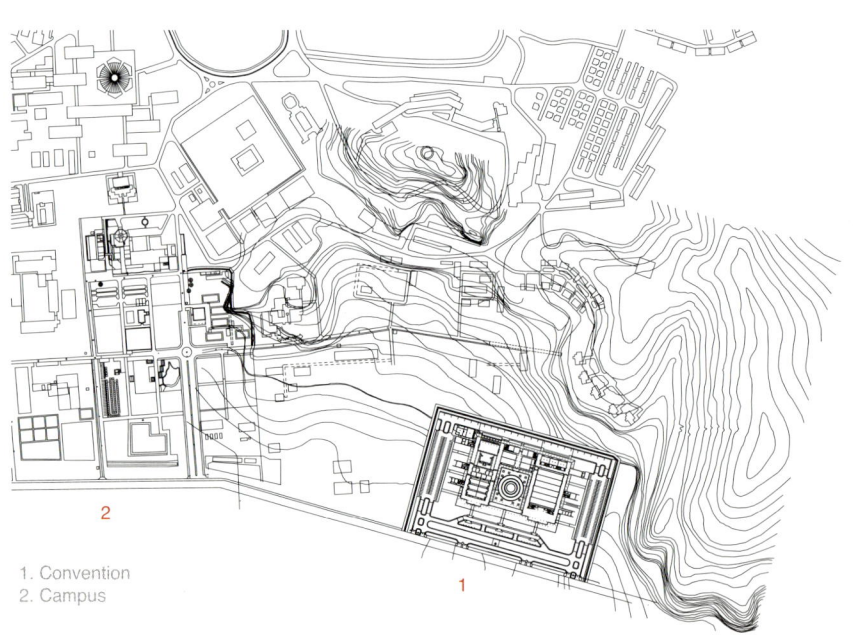

1. Convention
2. Campus

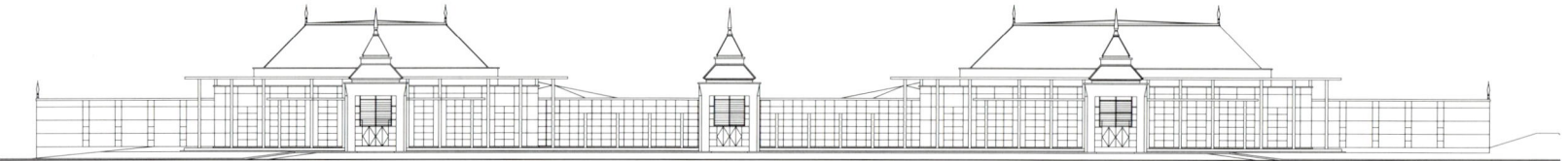

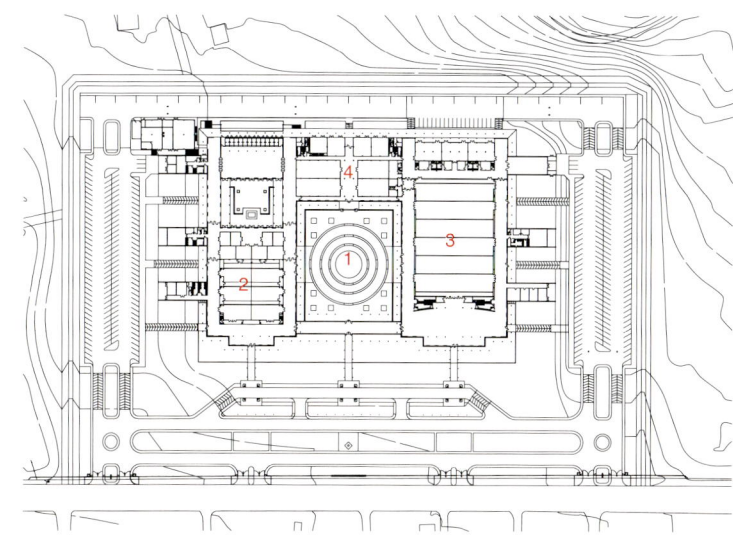

1. Activity plaza
2. Convention room
3. Convention hall
4. Meeting room

Main activity plaza

045

Henry B Thompson Building

R Sakran Punyatalung

Location :
Kasemsan 2, Rama I Road, Pathum Wan, Bangkok

Client :
Jim Thompson, The Thai Silk

Area : 1,000 sq.m.

Year : 2005-2006

The four-story multi-purpose Henry B Thompson Building, designed by Punyatalung and Ratchada Burunchai, was built on the new ground of the Jim Thompson House Museum compound. Constructed to support and facilitate the museum and the Jim Thompson Art Center, the building contains the William Warren Library and the art center office, along with Restaurateurs Sans Frontières and artist residences.

The architects carefully developed their design by considering both physical and abstract contexts such as Bangkok's tropical climate, uses of eco-friendly materials, harmony with its surroundings and the embracing of the structure as a new member of the Jim Thompson House compound. Importantly, the characteristics of the Jim Thompson Museum's Thai traditional house were thoroughly studied. The design vocabularies of the ancient Siamese architecture vernacular were transposed into the new building through the use of new materials and contemporary details.

The result was a clearly modern architecture, where various functionalities were accommodated into spaces arranged simply for easy circulation and control. The overall look is that of unpainted concrete, showing the material's truthfulness, accentuated by vertical lines of drainage pipes along with sun and wind shields. Rotatable teak walls, steel, aluminum and energy-saving glass play significant roles in formulating the building's exterior characteristics. The interior, on the other hand, shows its clarity with vertical spatial relationships. For instance, the solid ground-level walls form the museum's storage. Deep red elements, similar to the red regularly used for Jim Thompson Houses, help connect the new with the old; while the plant filled third-floor balcony resembles the beautiful traditional garden within the museum's quarter.

Though the new building is not actually connected to the land of the old compound, the symbolic connection is well maintained.

1. The Henry B Thompson Building
2. Jim Thompson's House
3. The Jim Thompson Art Center
4. The Thompson Bar and Restaurant

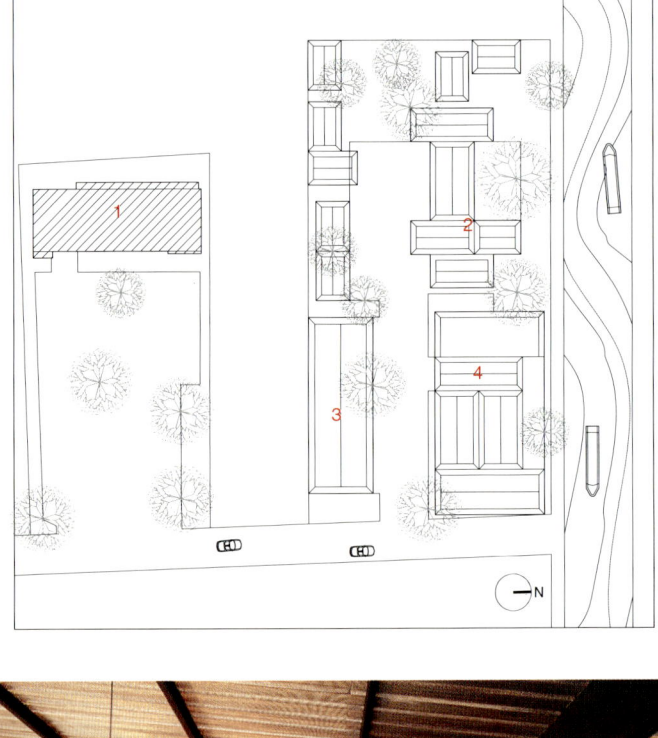

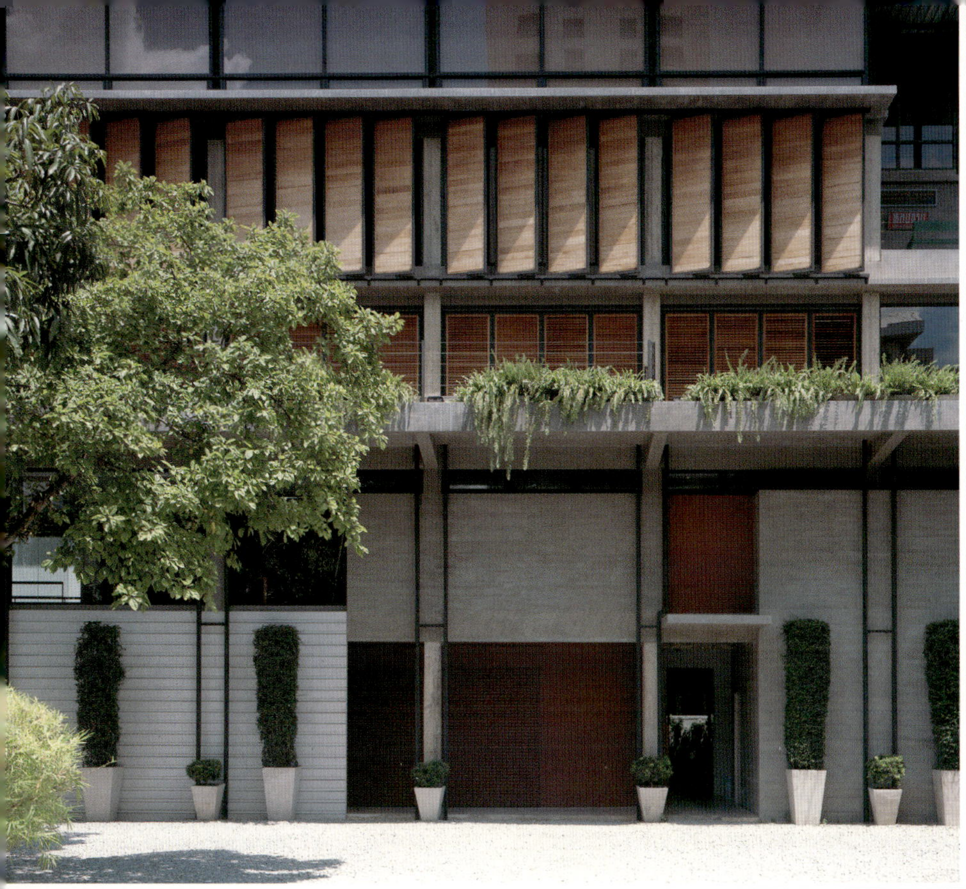

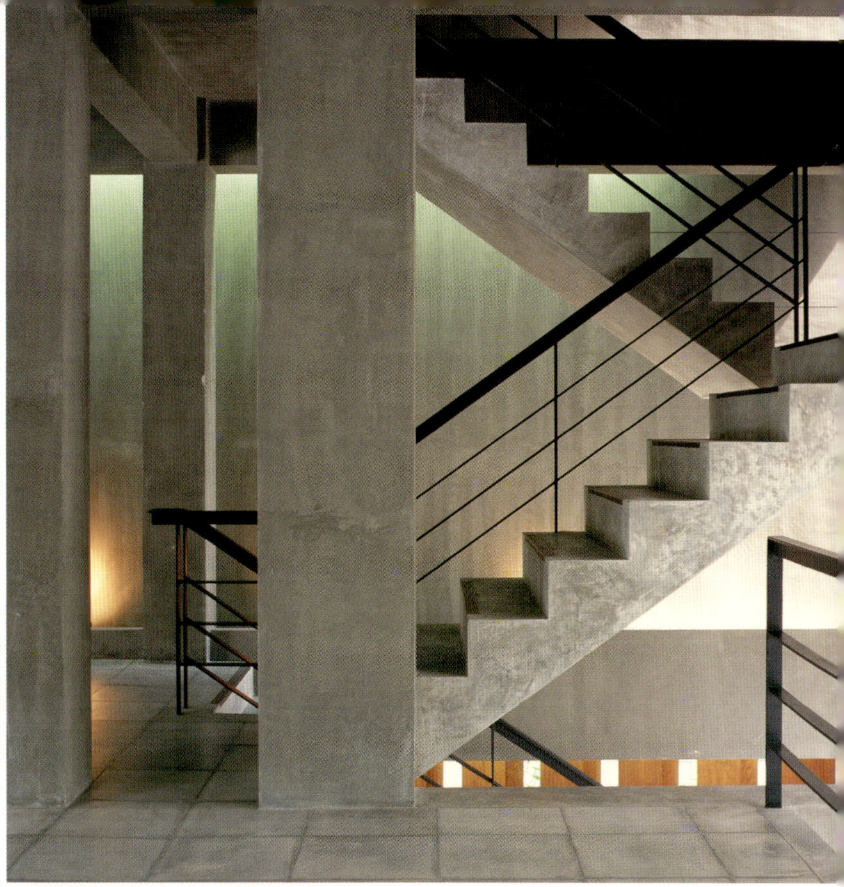

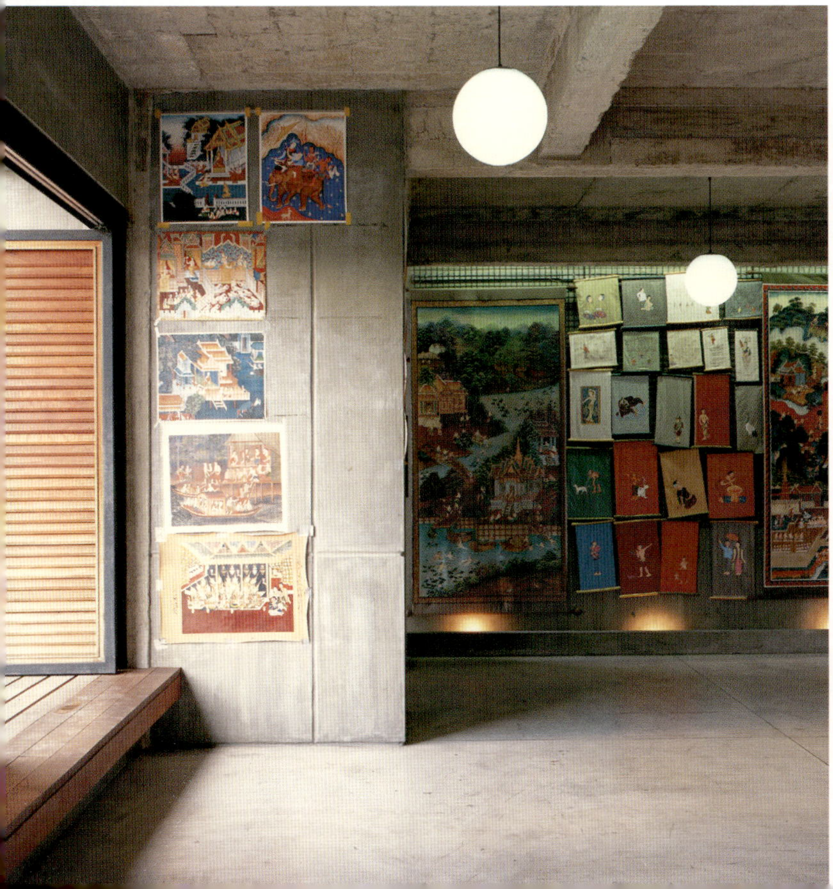

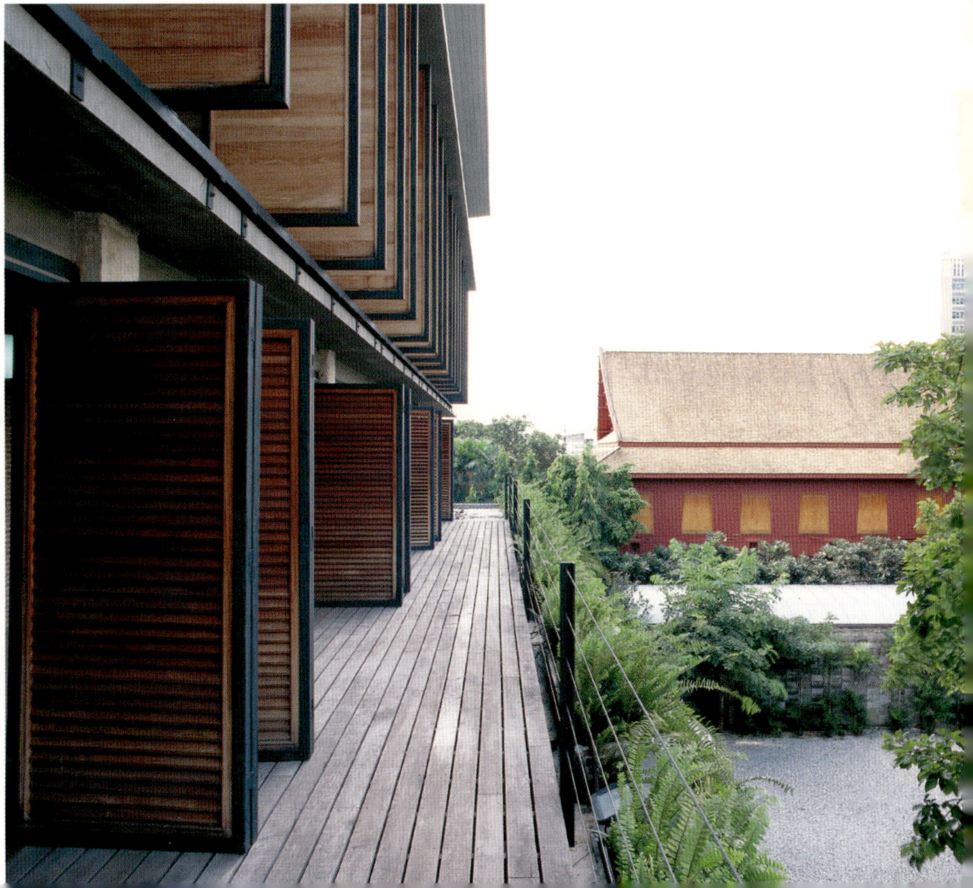

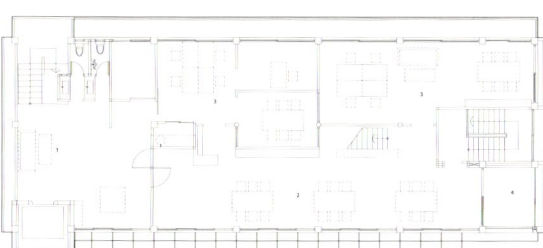

3rd floor

046

BU Landmark Complex   Architects 49

Location :
Vibhavadi Rangsit Road, Pathum Thani

Client :
Bangkok University

Area :
25,000 sq.m.

Year :
2006- 2009

This landmark complex originated from the university's desire to improve campus frontal access and provide students one of the finest facilities in the region.

The complex is composed of 4 buildings. The first two buildings are arranged rectangularly, yet offer a variety of visual planes through the use of uneven angle glazing. Together they contain functional space, including a seminar room and 1,500-seat auditorium. An open-air atrium links the two areas, where interwoven vertical flows such as the escalator and the elevator convey a sense of grandeur. Service cores are placed on the two side edges of the slab, opening a rear view to the entire west campus.

Two front edifices embrace the visionary image of the university through the art of architecture. Formed as a group of cut diamonds, the buildings metaphorically imply the crystalline body of student knowledge shaped by the education of this university.

All buildings stand separately on the ground, but are connected by a 300-car underground parking lot.

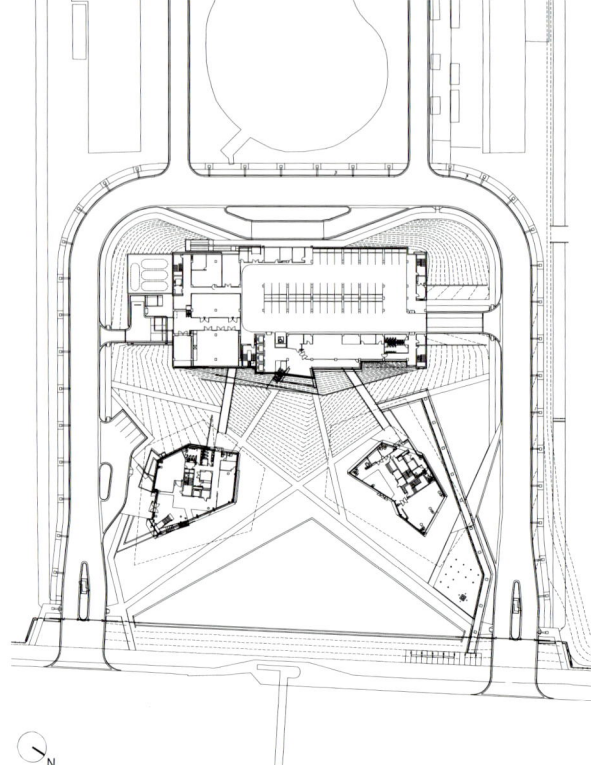

N

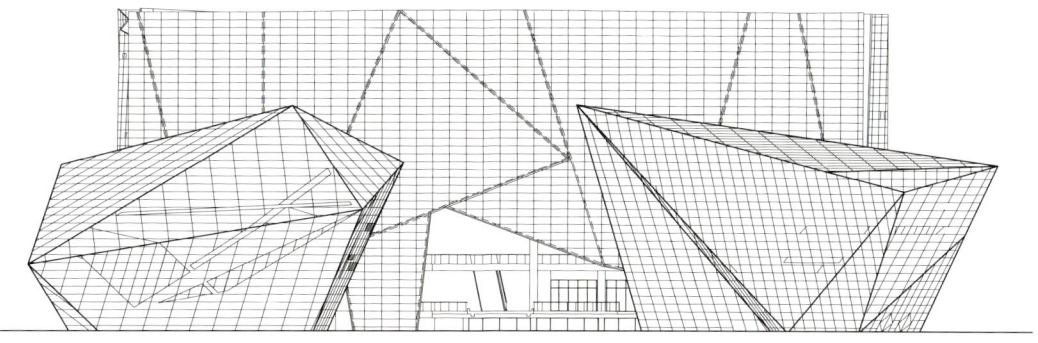

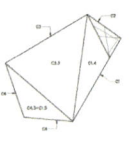

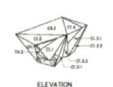

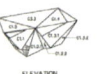

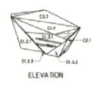

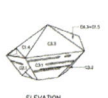

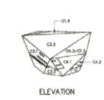

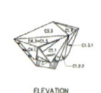

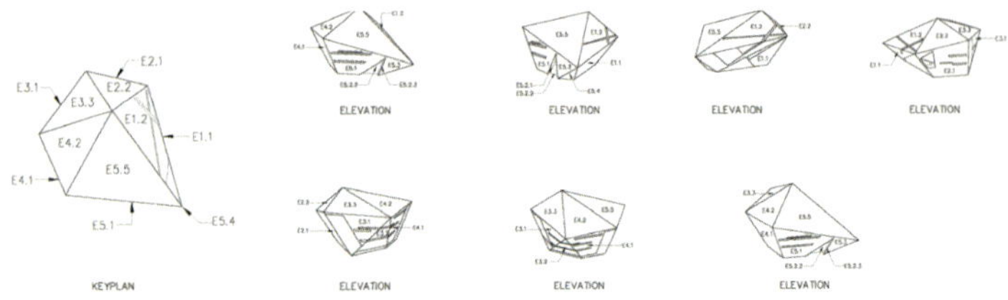

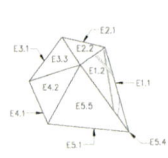

KEYPLAN
ELEVATION
ELEVATION
ELEVATION
ELEVATION
ELEVATION
ELEVATION
ELEVATION
ELEVATION
ELEVATION

E2.1
E3.1
E2.2
E3.3
E1.2
E1.1
E4.2
E5.5
E4.1
E5.1
E5.4
KEYPLAN
ELEVATION
ELEVATION
ELEVATION
ELEVATION
ELEVATION
ELEVATION
ELEVATION

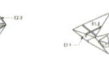

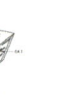

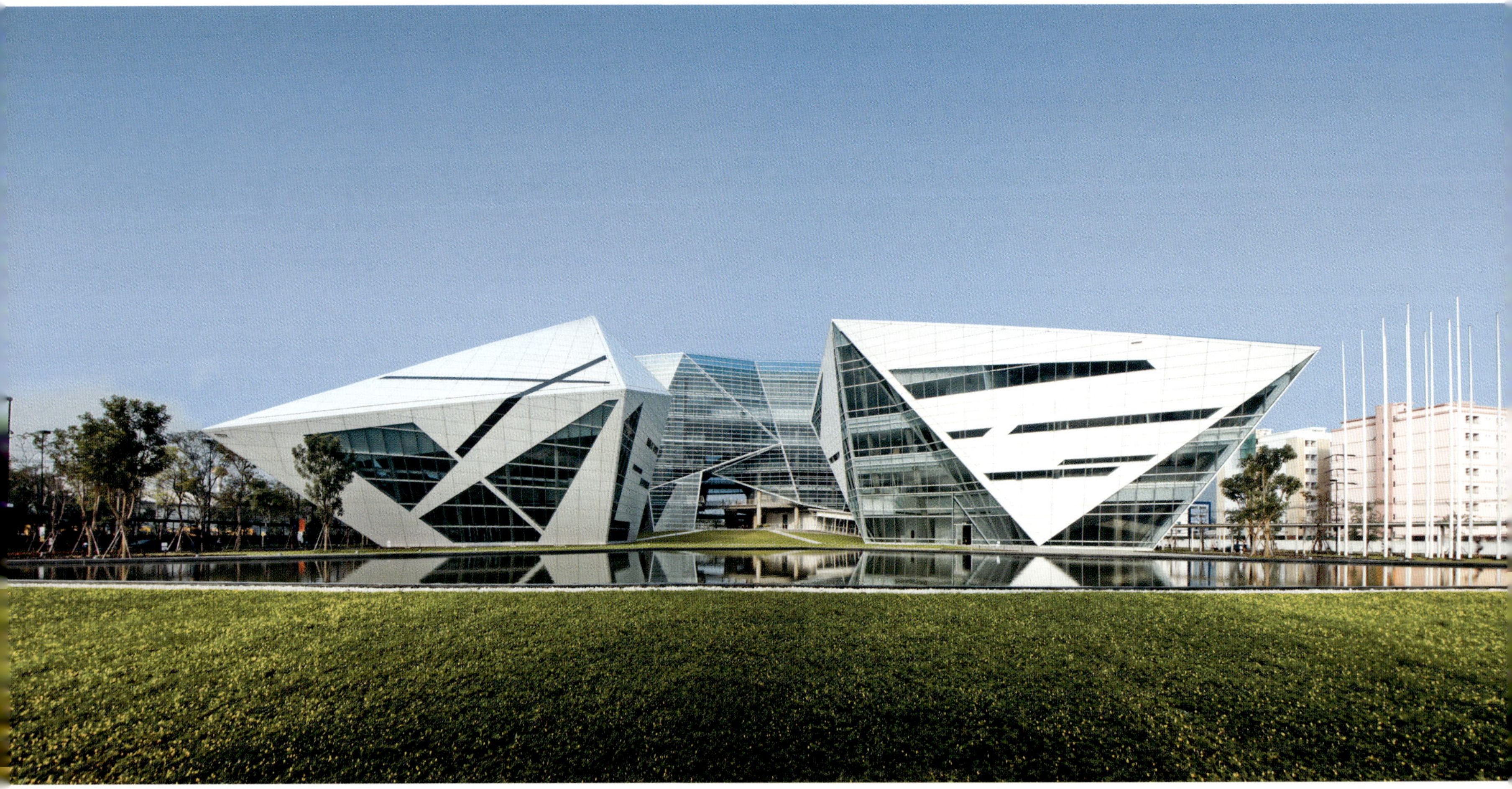

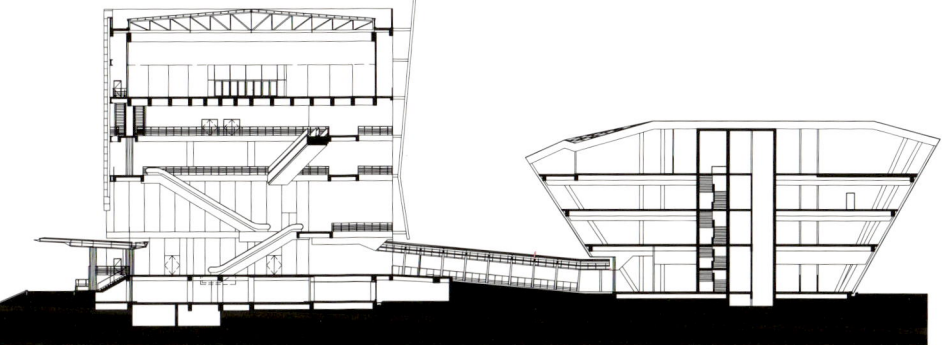

047

Arsom Silp Institute of the Arts and Development

Ashram of Community and Environmental Architect, Arsom Silp Institute of the Arts and Development

Location :
Rama II Road, Bang Khun Thian, Bangkok

Client :
Arsom Silp Institute of the Arts and Development

Area :
2,030 sq.m.

Year :
2006-2009

The Arsom Silp Institute of the Arts and Development is an alternative education institution offering graduate study programs. The Institute's mission is to teach human and spiritual beauty by pursuing ancestral wisdom and community service; which leads to self-understanding. Accordingly, the proposed Institute buildings should both serve distinctive learning activities and signify its unique identity.

The architectural compound is designed to encourage interaction and participation among all users. A number of informal meeting places are positioned throughout the 5 buildings, connected by wooden deck and walkway. Occupying 50% of building area, this series of semi-outdoor spaces is linked by both physical circulation and visual connectivity. The spaces are surrounded by a large grass forecourt and are intended to house multiple simultaneous activities.

The building design showcases a contemporary tropical architecture which responds aptly to the Thai climate. A hybrid energy-conscience system of minimal summer air-conditioning use and natural winter ventilation encourage energy conservation.

The landscape design, dominated by a large pound and dense trees, represent the concept of "landscape dominate architecture", existing in a calm and reflective natural harmony.

With a semi-random arrangement, high-pitch roofs and natural construction material (such as wood and palm leaf roof), the compound deliberately recalls a sense of contemporary vernacular.

Building in the midst of dense trees; an architectural existence in harmony with nature.

1. Architect studio
2. Workshop
3. Library
4. President room
5. Research department (2nd Phase)
6. Bamboo art gallery (2ng Phase)

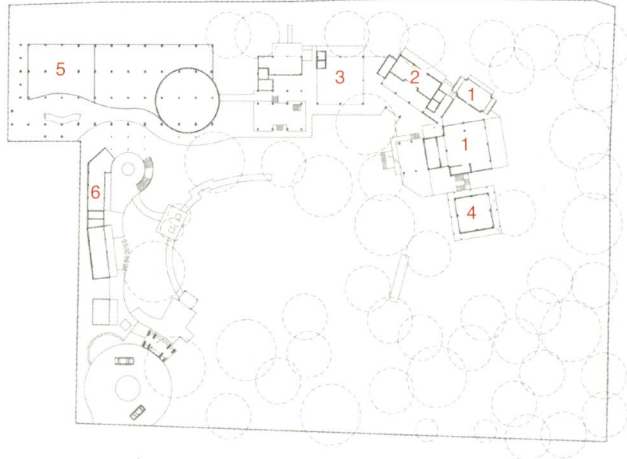

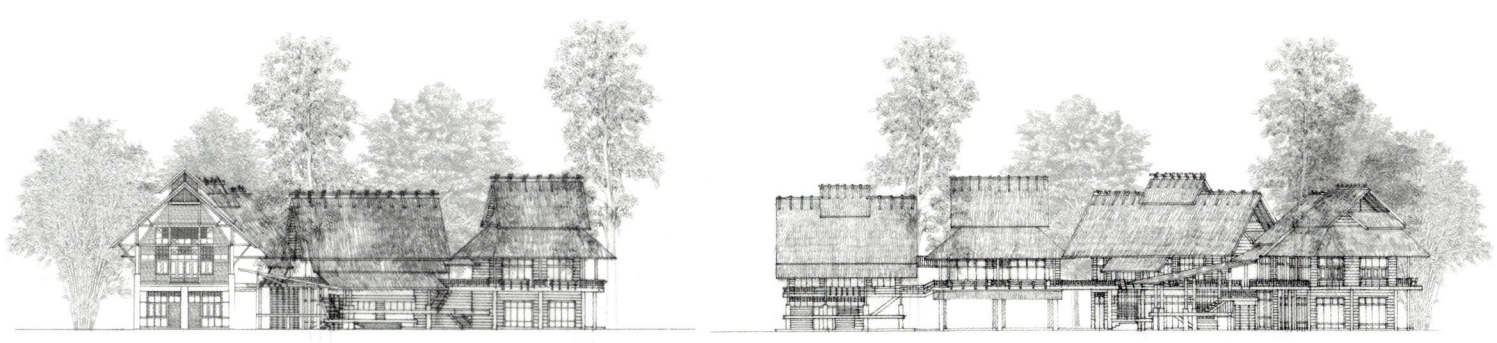

A predominent use of palm leaf roof and opened ground
floor recalls the sense of vernacular architecture.

The large open well space is planked by mezzanine office space encouraging open communication and visual contact for all staff in the architect studio.

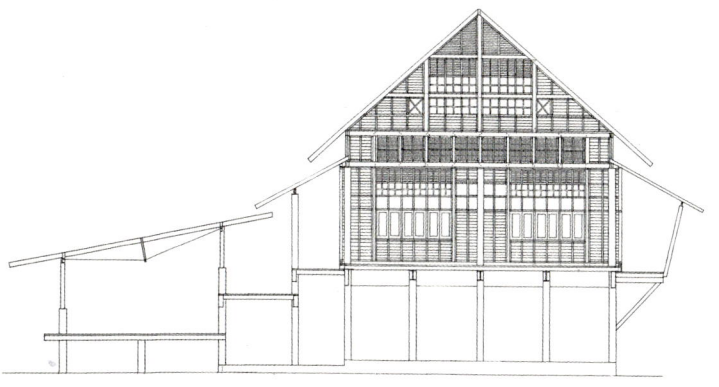

Main open-corridor, provides a picturesque sunset atmosphere.

'Chan Choom-Chon' (community deck) semi-outdoor spaces provided for learning activities and group meetings.

Three levels loft-like office space allow open views of the roof structure.

048

Dr. Arthit Urairat Building, Rangsit University

ARJ Studio

Location :
Muang-Ake Estate, Pathum Thani

Client :
Rangsit University

Area :
17,000 sq.m.

Year :
2002-2004

Constructed on the existing structure's foundation built in 1994, this 11-story edifice is a campus landmark. Its asymmetrical axis serves both as the main entrance and gateway to the second phase campus extension.

The most frequently used student and public services are provided at the easily-accessible ground level. This multi-functional atrium functions as prominent lobby, information area, registration office and bank. The semi-oval shaped roof stretches across a 3-story podium skin at the rear northern façade.

The louvered sun screen set behind the curtain walls and the curved, sheet metal roof act as sieves, filtering natural light into the structure and creating diverse light conditions that fluctuate with the time of the day and the season.

The building is equipped with sustainable, energy-efficient mechanical systems, providing ample natural light and ventilation. The overall massing of the podium creates a transition in scale between the library buildings to the north and the educational neighborhoods to the west. All materials and designs are carefully selected and integrated into the university's urban culture.

Detail of the slender shape louver that stretching across 3 stories.

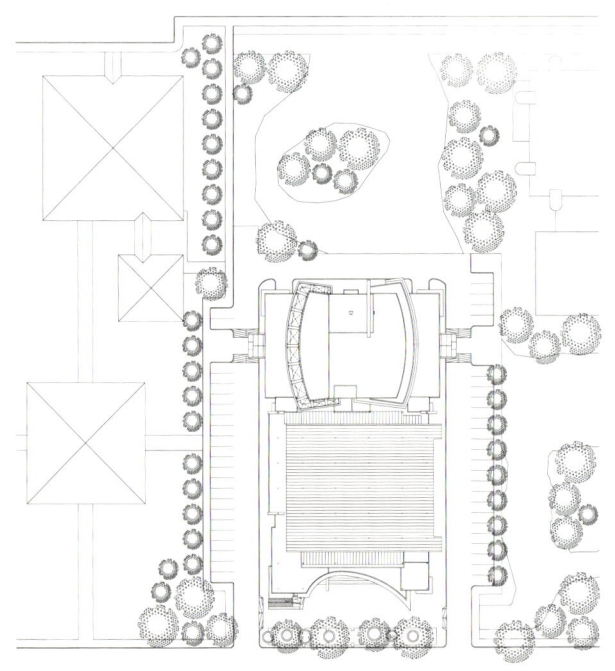

An aluminum shading devioce louvered as a horizontal line of tower.

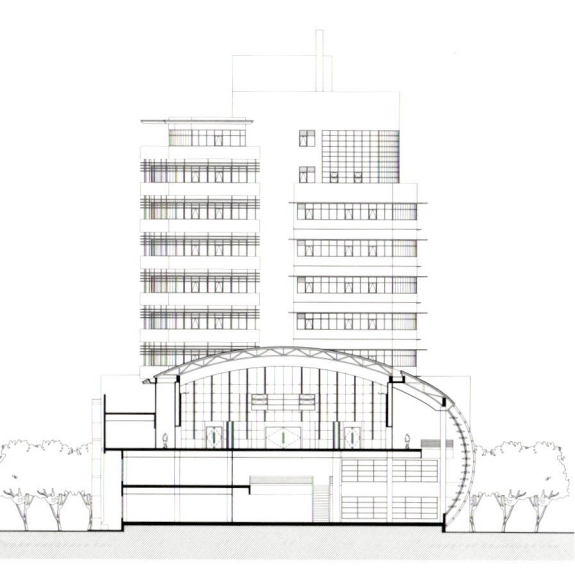

1. A non-symmetric curve wall as sexy shape above main frontage
2. Shading elements that form a fixed sunscreen louvered
3. Rectangular tiles finished on a precast concrete wall.

049

College of Medicine and Public Health

Geodesic Design

Location :
Ubon Ratchathani

Client :
Ubon Ratchathani University

Area :
9,050 sq.m.

Year :
2006-2009

The College of Medicine and Public Health Building project concept was to connect the College of Medicine and Public Health with the Ho Trai library while retaining the local Thai architecture of the Ubon Rajathanee building to the northeast. The design followed the library's square contour with Thai-styled architectural elements: traditional rectangle windows, a hip roof and floating columns. Surrounded by classrooms and the medical laboratory, space links the structures both functionally and visually. The open plan also impacts the ventilation, light, shade and shadow and strengthens the buildings' mechanical systems.

Locally produced materials such as the Ho Tri building's clay roof is core to the concept. Concrete blocks intermingled with steel form the classroom buildings' shell; providing a functional area while retaining the unique local heritage features for generations to enjoy.

1. Lecture hall
2. Medical laboratories
3. Office

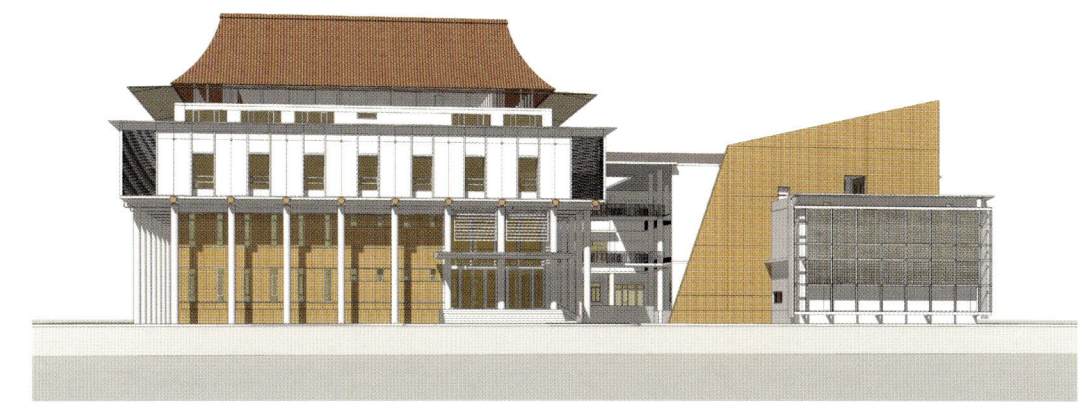

252

Bangkok University Admission and Information Center
OFFICE AT

Location : Kluaynamthai, Bangkok

Client : Bangkok University

Area : 1,612 sq.m.

Year : 2007

Bangkok University Admission and Information Center building is a mixed-use facility supporting a variety of programs and activities, including the Admission and Information Center, a student lounge and an 80-seat restaurant.

After designers evaluated all the site programs, the Information Center and student lounge were relocated to the upper level so they would be clearly visible from the main street. When these core offices were moved to the second floor, the resulting empty area was designated as open space to improve pedestrian circulation. The residual floor space was developed into a service zone and restaurant.

In order to complement the main street view and front campus facade, the building was folded.

A section of the student lounge was extended to serve as a restaurant first floor entrance approach and move the student area near the reflecting pool.

The building site is in front of the Bangkok University's main campus. The second floor information center is linked by stairs directly to the public plaza. The stairs are divided into two levels to reduce stair height. The first level uses the same material as the plaza, the second level is designed for user can walk comfortably.

To support users from different directions, the building plans provided an interior staircase with a skylight. There is rear handicapped ramp used to connect the building with the landscape and nearby building. A black granite reflecting pool is set in front of the building to comfort and relax patrons.

The cantilever box at student lounge is covered with a double layered skin. The inner layer is transparent glass; the outer skin is perforated aluminum panel which continues from the interior space to cover the cantilever box. The double layer skin is opaque during the day, providing student lounge privacy and transparent at night, providing security.

The main material is painted plastered brick wall. The admission center is framed with concrete and opaque glass to communicate with the street. The other functions are covered with tinted glass.

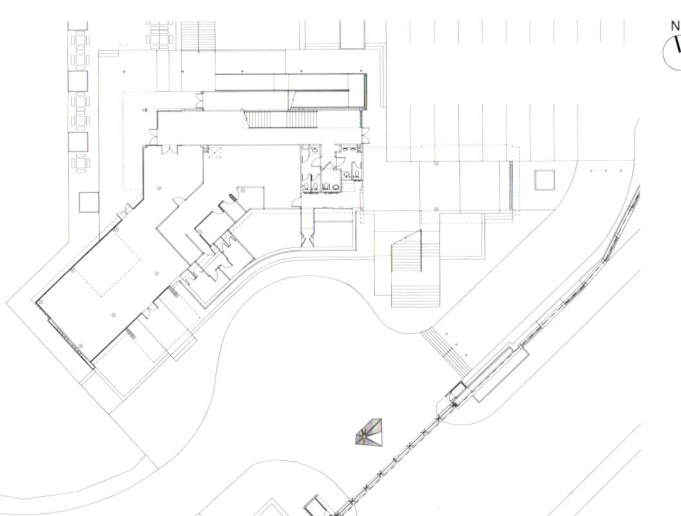

N

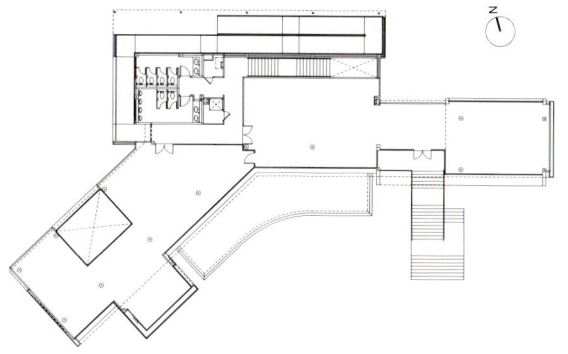

Bangkok University International College and Art Gallery
OFFICE AT

Location : Kluaynamthai, Bangkok
Client : Bangkok University
Area : 3,641 sq.m.
Year : 2004- 2006

The activities axis is the line across which most activities flow. The project site, a triangle-shaped piece of land at the one end of this axis, connects to the main road on this axis. To continue movement from the main axis and make the university more dynamic, designers continued the activities axis inside the new building through to the outside university as well.

The building design occupies the maximum site area, simply and strictly following the required zoning envelope to create a building with maximum volume. Continuing the activities axis by reducing some first floor volume along the axis will create a new gateway to the university.

To overcome the challenge of dynamic, disparate activities, the plan produces new space between the visible hole, called the event stair; a flexible function that eliminates the traditional distinction between the gallery and other programs.

Because of modern site limitations, cultural change and user diversity, buildings today must support a variety of programs in the same structure. This building meets the challenge. It is a mix-used building, which maintains an international college and art gallery.

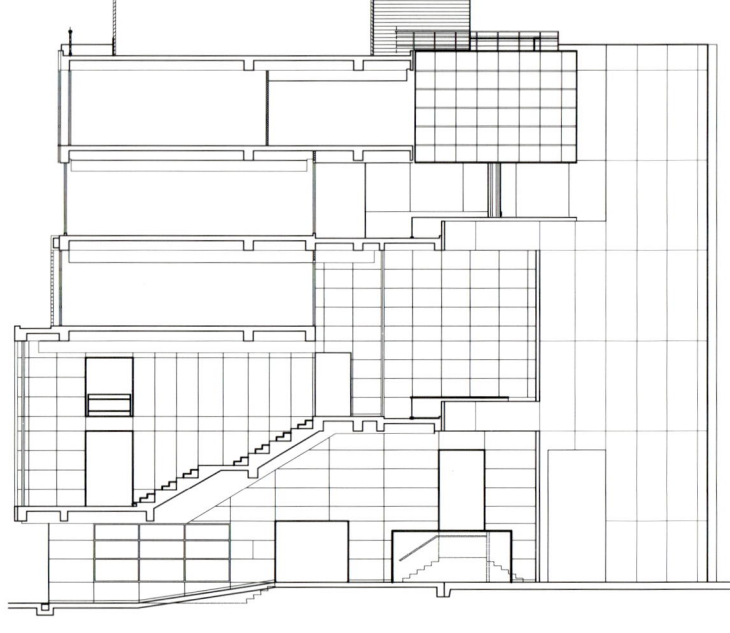

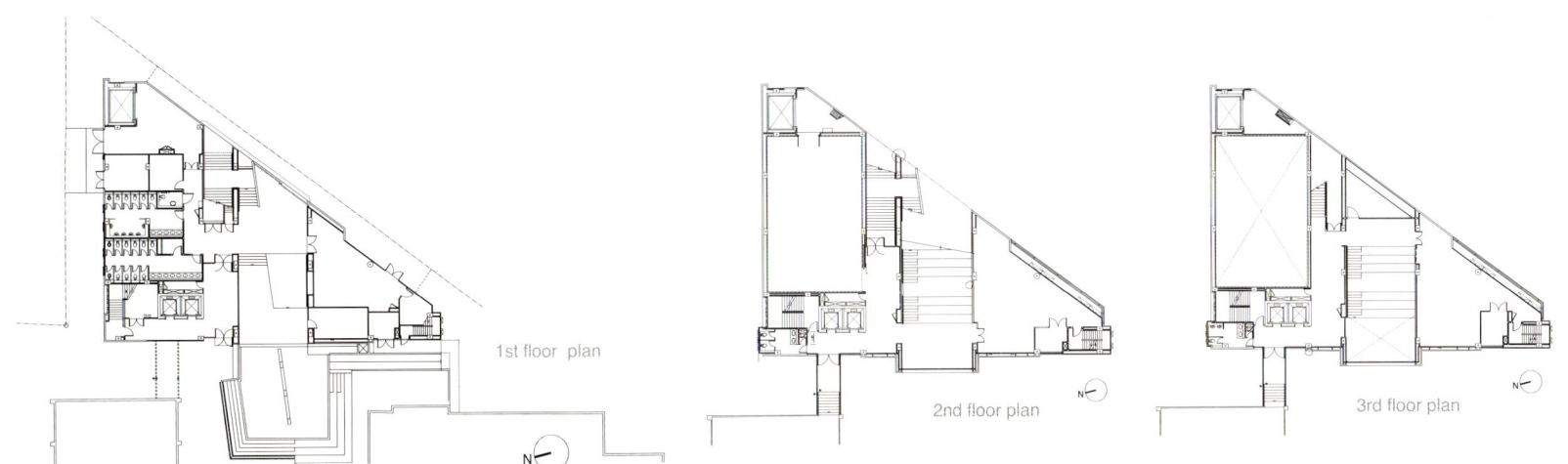

1st floor plan

N

2nd floor plan

N

3rd floor plan

N

College of Music, Mahidol University
Tonsilp Studio

Location :
Buddamonton 4 Road, Salaya,
Nakhon Pathom

Client :
College of Music, Mahidol
University

Area :
19,534 sq.m.

Year :
1997-2005

This project has many primary entrance points. The site plan emphasizes the main open space that joins every building and entrance. This space faces a pond to the north, creating a line of sight to the Mahidol University campus, and connects to footpaths. The west side is designed to be the main entrance from the campus. Currently, this area is being redesigned as a park connecting to the new College of Music building.

The concept is 'key space', also known as 'semi-outdoor space'. Since enclosed space is viewed as 'black' and open space as 'white', the most important element that incorporated into the work was a focus on the grey space that flows between the two. Grey space is created in varying values and many shades to compose continuity and connectedness; to set off; to provide access; to acknowledge or not. It is the nucleus that links the exterior and the interior. This connectivity is created architecturally by developing a matrix of points, lines, planes that spill out into the grounds. Breezes blow and dust particles coat the grey space. In architecture, 'conceptual space' flows down to and cloaks the surroundings, then, flows back and forth, continually. In other words, conceptual space blurs the borders between exterior and interior, blending them together.

This project aimed to establish 'a friendly, charming musical community' by creating a connected, flowing, multi-purpose space as the central component of the complex. Designers made an effort to achieve 'unity in complexity', one of the basic approaches in Eastern thinking; to create 'quiet' spaces among the dynamic building elements that come alive with the presence of people and the sounds of music. This is how imagination underlies the use of grey space.

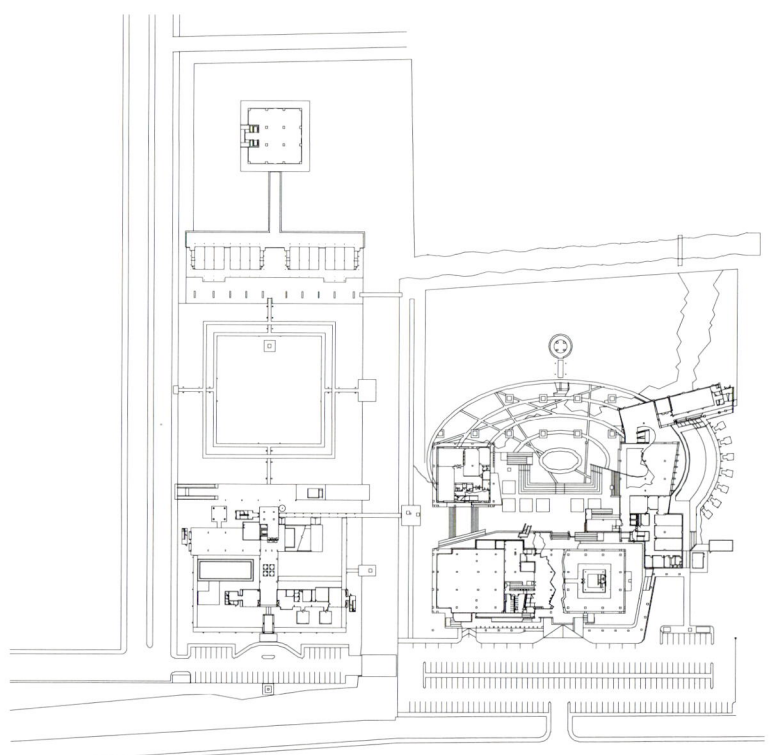

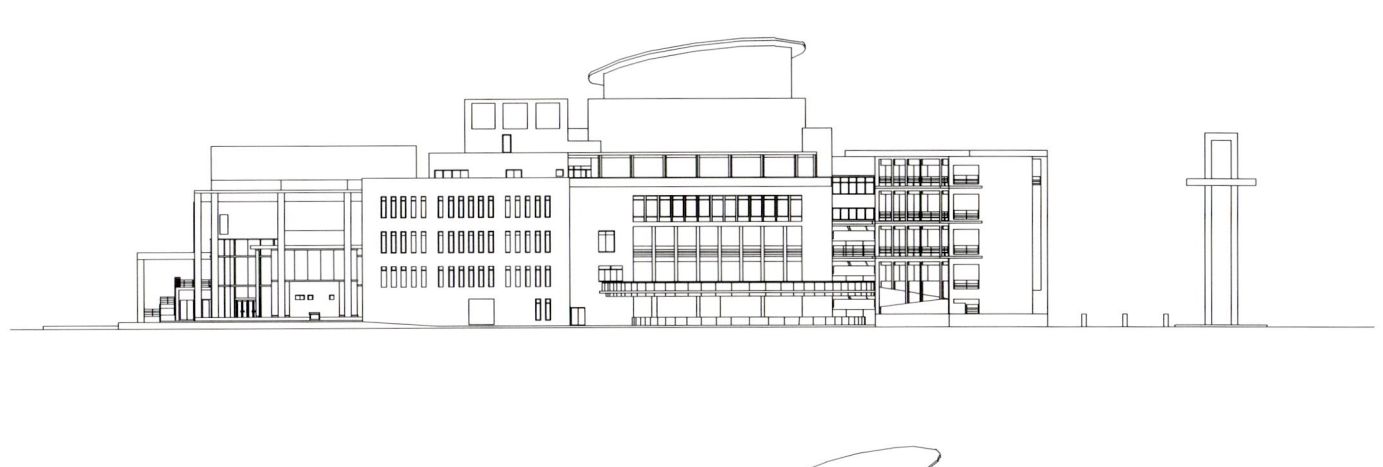

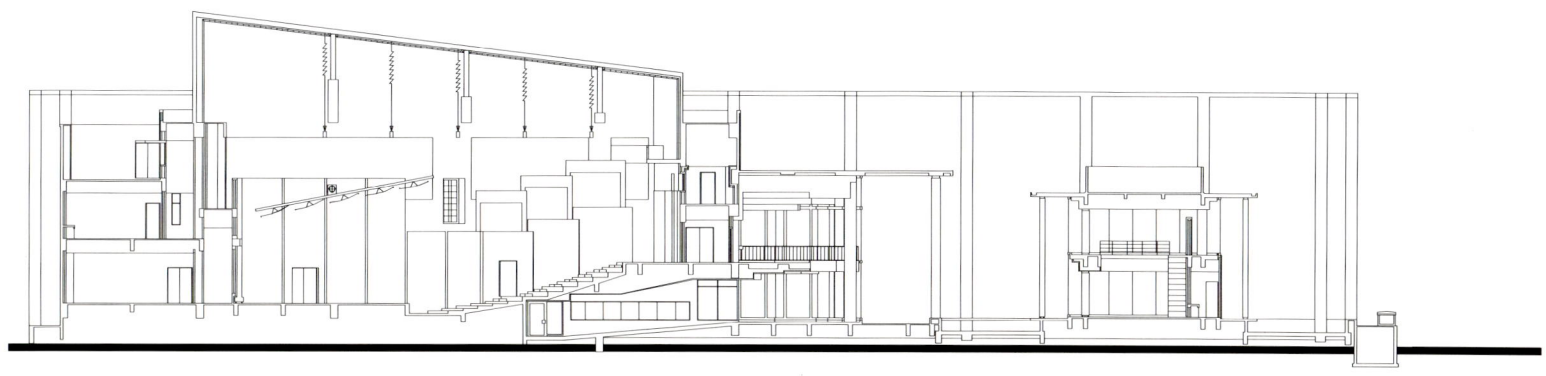

Appendix

MODERN ARCHITECTURE IN THAILAND 001

Index of Firms and Projects

Airports of Thailand
Suvarnabhumi International Airport

alchemist design studio
4C House

amA design studio
Baan Sukhumvit 40
Chai Tour Office

ARbay
Architect Council of Thailand
Issara@42

Archer Architect
Century the Movie Plaza

Architects 49
Baan Bang Sarae
Baan Pracha Uthit
Baan Windmill
BU Landmark Complex
Central Plaza Khon Kaen
Energy Complex
King Power Complex
Royal Archive
SCG Experience
The 49 Terrace
The Emporio

Architects & Associates
Baan Suriyan Chandra
Crew Training Center (Renovation)
Operation Center
Satin Textile Worker Multi-Family Housing
Suvarnabhumi Honda Automobile

Architecture and Interior
Rama Nine Gardens Residences
Thailand Elite Head Quarters

ARJ Studio
Dr. Arthit Urairat Building, Rangsit University
Stepwise Group Headquarter

**Ashram of Community & Environmental Architect,
Arsom Silp Institute of the Arts and Development**
Arsom Silp Institute of the Arts and Development
Bann Huen Tham (The House of Dharma)
Community Organization Development Institute (CODI)

begray
X2 Resort Samui

BOON DESIGN
Kauphanichanon's Residence

Composition A
Asawanonda Residence
The Oriental Fine Art

Deca Atelier
Casa de Umbrella
Osotspa Building 3
Osotspa Canteen

Department of ARCHITECTURE
Sala Phuket
Sun One

Design 103 International
Holiday Inn Pattaya Hotel
Le Meridien Hotel, Bangkok
Siam Paragon Shopping Center

Design Concept
Suvarnabhumi Airport Rail Link and City Air Terminal

DUANGRIT BUNNAG ARCHITECT
X2 Kui Buri
Residence Sriracha

dwp
Uawithya Showroom

EAST architects
Amanta
Iudia

Faculty of Architecture, Chulalongkorn University
Exhibition Gallery, Chulalongkorn University

Form Architect
Workpoint Studio Village

Geodesic Design
Collage of Medicine and Public Health

Great Architect
Amari Residences Hua Hin Street Side Restaurant
Best Western Premier Amaranth Suvarnabhumi Airport Hotel

Habita
Samui International Airport
Yaiya Hua Hin

HASSELL
Sala @ Sathorn

HB Design
The Heights

IDIN Architects
C House
Phuket Gateway

Interior Architecture 103
The First Royal Factory at Fang the Museum

JUNSEKINO Architecture + Design
Nature House

Khiensak Seangklieng
The Briza Beach Resort and Spa
Local Hero

KTGY Inter-Associates
The Retreat

Metric
Six Senses Hideaway

Minimaxist
Chang House

OFFICE AT
Bangkok University Admission and Information Center
Bangkok University International College and Art Gallery

Ongsa Architects
Manarom Hospital
PM Center Office Building

OPENBOX
Plearnwan
U House

Palmer & Turner (Thailand)
Grand Millennium Sukhumvit
Interchange 21
The Park Chidlom
Watermark Chaophraya, Chaophraya River

Plan Associates
Bank of Thailand Headquarter
Practika Factory
Prince of Songkhla University International Convention Center
Red Mountain Golf Club
Sheraton Krabi Beach Resort

Plankrich
2BR
Baan Jew
Baan Suan Nonsee
Compact House
Maze
Mo Rooms
The Office Plus

Pornchai Boonsom Architect
MnG House

R Sakran Punyatalung
Henry B Thompson Building

Robert G. Boughey and Associates
Q. House Lumpini Park
Intanate House

ROOF
Cape Sienna Phuket Hotel
The Bell

Smit Associates
A Camouflage House

Spacetime Architect
Baan Sam Kanan (3 Parallels House)

Supermachine Studio
Harbormall
Prakit House

TEAC
Bangkok Christian Hospital (Extension)

The Office of Bangkok Architects
Ayodhaya Links Clubhouse
Banyan Golf Clubhouse
Esplanade & Ratchadalai Theater
K Village
Mini Showroom
Veranda Chiangmai the High Resort

Thonsilp Studio
College of Music, Mahidol University

VaSLab
Bracket House
Bunker House
Deviated House
Honda Big Wing

alchemist design studio (2001)

201/1 Charan Sanit Wong 63, Charan Sanit Wong Road,
Bang Phlat, Bangkok 10700 Thailand
srisak_ph@yahoo.com

Srisak Phattanawasin

Archer Architect (1991)

236-238-240-242, Asoke-Din Daeng Road, Bang Kapi,
Huai Khwang, Bangkok 10310 Thailand
archerarchitect@yahoo.com

Jiradach Danpoe
Penpak Ngamsatain

Architecture and Interior (2001)

Chalerm Phrakiat 34, Nong Bon, Prawet, Bangkok 10250 Thailand
kovit.s@aiodesigns.com, www.aiodesigns.com

Kovit Suriyporn

amA Design Studio (2002)

84/5-6 Sukhumvit 62, Sukhumvit Road, Bang Chak,
Phra Khanong, Bangkok 10260 Thailand
ama@amadesignstudio.net, www.amadesignstudio.net

Chatchai Assawasukee
Sawanya Srikulnath
Korakot Prisawong

Architects 49 (1983)

81 Sukhumvit 26, Sukhumvit Road, Khlong Ton, Khlong Toei,
Bangkok 10110 Thailand
a49@a49.com, www.a49.com

Prabhakorn Vadanyakul	Managing Director
Suwat Vasapinyokul	Deputy Managing Director
Pichai Wongwaisayawan	Deputy Managing Director

ARJ Studio (2001)

300/135 Phahon Yothin 87, Phahon Yothin Road
Lam Luk Ka, Pathum Thani 12130 Thailand
info@arjstudio.com, www.arjstudio.com

Janejud Sri-aroon	Principal
Supukkin Limcharoen	Senior Architect

ARbay (2006)

31st FL., Bangkok Insurance Building, South Sathon Road,
Thung Mahamek, Sathon, Bangkok 10120 Thailand
info@arbay.co.th, www.arbay.co.th

Prakit Phananuratana

Architects & Associates (1990)

9/F RS Tower 121/37 Ratchadaphisek Road, Bangkok 10400 Thailand
arch.asso@gmail.com, www.AandA.co.th

Ashram of Community and Environmental Architects, Arsom Silp Institute of the Arts and Development (2005)

9/12 Moo 5 Soi 33, Rama II Road, Thakam, Bang Khun Thian
Bangkok 10150 Thailand
arch@arsomsilp.in.th

Theeraphon Niyom — Design Director

⌄ Begray (1999)
2/4 Sukhumvit 28, Sukhumvit Road, Khlong Ton, Khlong Toei,
Bangkok 10110 Thailand
thebegray@gmail.com, www.begray.com

Jakarin Aksravadeewat
Viwat Kunalangkarn
Chaned Aksravadeewat

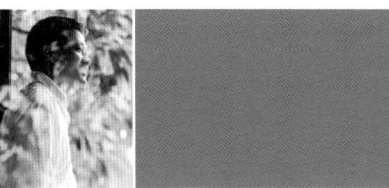

⌄ BOON DESIGN (2010)
113 Soi Praditmanutham19, Praditmanutham Road,
Lat Phrao, Bangkok 10230 Thailand
boon_design@yahoo.com

Boonlert Hemvijitraphan

⌄ Composition A (1995)
172/20 Preedeepanomyong 20, Sukumvit 71, Sukhumvit Road,
Phra Khanong Nua, Wattana, Bangkok 10110 Thailand
compo@compo-a.com, www.compo-a.com

Metee Rasameevijitpisal
Apiradee Kasemsook
Nathiya Thongmee

⌄ Design 103 International (1968)
9th Floor, Asoke Tower Office Building
219/28-31 Soi Asoke, Sukhumvit 21, Sukhumvit Road,
Khlong Toei Nua, Wattana, Bangkok 10110 Thailand
office@d103group.com, www.d103group.com

Ramese Kanjanapokin   President

⌄ Deca Atelier
4/7 Senabadee Building 1, 1st Floor, Phahon Yothin 11,
Phahon Yothin Road, Samsen Nai, Phaya Thai,
Bangkok 10400 Thailand
interior@deca-atelier.com

Somchai Jongsaeng

⌄ Department of ARCHITECTURE (2004)
3 Soi Premier 1 Branch 14 Srinakarindra Road,
Prawet, Bangkok 10250 Thailand
dept.of.arch@gmail.com, www.departmentofarchitecture.co.th

Amata Luphaiboon
Twitee Vajrabhaya Teparkum

⌄ Design Concept (1990)
88/29 Soi Timland, Ngam Wongwan Road,
Nonthaburi 11000 Thailand
dca@designconceptarchitect.com, www.designconceptarchitect.com

Kiatsakul Ketmayura, AIA   President
Vineeta Kalyanamitra   Managing Director
Watanawong Snidvongs   Design Director

⌄ DUANGRIT BUNNAG ARCHITECT (1998)
989 Floor 28 Unit A2, B3 Siam Tower, Rama I Road,
Pathum Wan, Bangkok 10330 Thailand
office@dbalp.com, www.dbalp.com

Duangrit Bunnag

⌄ dwp (1994)
The Dusit Thani Building Level 11, Unit A, 946 Rama IV Road,
Bangkok 10500 Thailand
thailand@dwp.com, www.dwp.com

Brenton Mauriello
Scott Whittaker
Sarinrath Kamolratanapiboon

⊗ EAST Architects (2004)

321/53-54 Nang Linchi Road, Yan Nawa, Bangkok 10500 Thailand
eastarchitects@eastarchitects.com, www.eastarchitects.com

Pirast Pacharaswate

⊗ Form Architect (1991)

9/29 Phahon Yothin 44, Phahon Yothin Road, Sena Nikhom,
Chatuchak, Bangkok 10900 Thailand
form_arc@yahoo.com

Suthit Wangrungarun

⊗ Faculty of Architecture Chulalongkorn University

Faculty of Architecture Chulalongkorn University,
Phayathai Road, Bangkok 10300 Thailand
www.archdept.com

Vira Sachakul
Sarayut Supsook
Chaiboon Sirithanawat

⊗ Geodesic Design (1991)

77/48 Soi Lat Phrao 1, Lat Phrao Road, Lat Yao,
Chatuchak, Bangkok 10900 Thailand
geobkk@geodesicdesign.co.th, www.geodesicdesign.co.th

Somboon Sudmaksri
Karp Boonthavi

⊗ Great Architect (2005)

1055/875 State Tower, 37th Floor, Silom Road,
Bang Rak, Bangkok 10500 Thailand
cgd@cgdinter.com, www.cgdinter.com

Sopit Sucharitkul
Arthit Lawsakul
Hemarat Changkeaw

⊗ Habita (1980)

408/16 Rama V Road, Dusit, Bangkok 10300 Thailand
contact@habitaarchitects.com, www.habitaarchitects.com

Krisda Rochanakorn   Principal
Pisit Sayampol   Principal

⊗ HASSELL (1995)

18F, K Tower, Sukhumvit 21, Sukhumvit Road, Khlong Toei Nua
Watthana, Bangkok 10110 Thailand
bangkok@hassell.co.th, www.hassell.com.au

Peter Skinner   Managing Director
Teerachai Manomaiphibul   Principal
Tanya Suvannapong   Principal

⊗ HB Design (1995)

16th fl, Unit 1603 The Millenia Tower, 62 Langsuan Road,
Patumwan, Bangkok 10330 Thailand
dennis@hbdesign.biz, www.hbdesign.biz

Dennis Stanfill

⊗ IDIN Architects (2004)

2 Sutthisan Winitchai Yaek1 Road, Din Daeng,
Bangkok 10400 Thailand
idin@idinarchitects.com, www.idinarchitects.com

Jeravej Hongsakul

Khiensak Seangklieng
Faculty of Architecture and Planning,
Thammasat University, Rangsit Center, 99 Moo 18, Khlong Nueng,
Khlong Luang, Pathumthani 12121 Thailand
khiensak@yahoo.com, www.ap.tu.ac.th

Interior Architecture 103 (1995)
14th Fl., Asoke Towers Office Building, Sukhumvit 21, Sukhumvit Road,
Khlong Toei Nua, Wattana, Bangkok 10110 Thailand
office@ia103.com, www.ia103.com

Ramese Kanjanapokin   President
Korakoth Kunalungkarn   Executive Vice President
Supathra Punsiri   Vice President

JUNSEKINO Architecture + Design (2008)
157 Soi 4/1 Seri 9, Rama IX Road, Suan Luang,
Bangkok 10250 Thailand
Sekin_o@hotmail.com, www.junsekinoarchitect.

Jun Sekino
Thissana Leelahapant

KTGY Inter-Associates (1991)
32nd Floor, Sorachai Building, Sukhumvit 63, Sukhumvit Road,
Khlong Ton Nua, Wattana, Bangkok 10110 Thailand
bd1@ktgyinterassoc.com, www.ktgyinterassoc.com

Tanitpong Chalermpanth   Chairman/Executive Principal
Sunantapat Chalermpanth   Chairman/Executive Principal
Peerayos Amatayakul   Executive Principal

Metric (1973)
3 Soi Premier 1 Branch 14 Srinakarindra Road,
Prawet, Bangkok 10250 Thailand
metric@metric.co.th

Amata Luphaiboon
Revaree Nophaket
Twitee Vajrabhaya Teparkum

Minimaxist (2004)
999/31 Soi 3 Pracha Uthit Road, Samsen Nork,
Huai Khwang, Bangkok 10320 Thailand
minimax_d@yahoo.com, www.mimmaxist.com

Vichate Tawatnantachai

OFFICE AT (2002)
61/56 2nd Floor, Soi Taveemitr 8, Rama IX Road,
Huai Khwang, Bangkok 10310 Thailand
contact@officeat.com, www.officeat.com

Surachai Akekapobyotin
Juthathip Techachumreon

Ongsa Architect (1990)
35/138 Soi Apaphirom, Ratchadaphisek Road,
Chatuchak, Bangkok 10900 Thailand
ongsa@ongsa.co.th, www.ongsa.co.th

Chalay Kunawong

OPENBOX (2004)
29/1 Piya Place Building, 17AB 17th floor, Lang Suan Road,
Lumpini, Bangkok 10300 Thailand
openbox@openbox.in.th, www.openbox.in.th

Ratiwat Suwannatrai
Wannaporn Suwannatrai

⌃ **Palmer & Turner (Thailand)** (1989)
231/9 Bangkok Cable Building II, 3rd Floor, Soi Sarasin,
Ratchadamri Road, Lumpini, Pathum Wan, Bangkok 10330 Thailand
ptthai@p-t-group.net, www.p-t-group.com

Sern Vithespongse   Director
Paween Kobboon   Director

⌄ **Pornchai Boonsom Architect** (1992)
288 Srivara Road, Soi Lat Phrao 94, Wang Thonglang,
Bangkok 10310 Thailand
pornchai_boonsom@yahoo.co.th, www.thelastdesing.com

Pornchai Boonsom
Kitti Raykhuntod

⌄ **ROOF** (1999)
100/999 Moo5 Rasada Road, Muang, Phuket 83000 Thailand
architect@roof.co.th, www.roof.co.th

⌄ **Plan Associates** (1989)
64 Sathon 10, North Sathon Road, Bangkok 10500 Thailand
plan@planassociates.co.th, www.planassociates.co.th

Boonrit Kordilokrat
Praditchya Singharaj

⌃ **R Sakran Punyatalung** (2004)
16 Phahol Yothin 33, Phahol Yothin Road, Bangkok 10900 Thailand
r.sakran@gmail.com, www.flickr.com/photos/sakran/

R Sakran Punyatalung

⌃ **Smit Associates** (1994)
168 Nakhon Sawan Road, Wat Sommanas,
Pom Prap Sattru Phai, Bangkok 10100 Thailand
oando4you@yahoo.com

Smit Vajaranant

⌄ **Plankrich** (2005)
25 Soi 13 Sirimankalacharn Road, Suthep,
Muang Chiang Mai 50200 Thailand
tuiiut@hotmail.com, www.plankrich.com

Tanit Choomsang
Khwanchai Suthamsao
Sakchai Thongphanchang

⌃ **Robert G. Boughey and Associates** (1973)
47 Soi Thonglor 23, Sukhumvit 55, Sukhumvit Road,
Khlong Ton Nua, Wattana, Bangkok 10110 Thailand
boughey@loxinfo.co.th, www.rgbarchitects.com

Robert G.Boughey

⌃ **Spacetime Architect** (2004)
F4 32 Soi Soonvijai 8(3), Petchaburi Road,
Huai Khwang, Bangkok 10320 Thailand
admin@spacetime.co.th, www.spacetime.co.th

Kanika R'kul Founder + Managing Director

The Office of Bangkok Architects (1994)
9 Soi Chidlom, Ploen Chit Road, Lumpini, Pathum Wan,
Bangkok 10330 Thailand
oba@bangkokarchitect.com, www.bangkokarchitect.com

Smith Obayawat   Principal
Waroon Limpchalerm   Executive director

Supermachine Studio (2003)
57/7 Chokchairuammit 16/13, Vibhavadi Rangsit Road,
Jompol, Chatuchak, Bangkok 10900 Thailand
supermachinestudio@gmail.com, http://supermachine.wordpress.com

Pitupong Chaowakul   Principal

TEAC (1976)
138/1 Soi Vibhavadi 2, Vibhavadi Rangsit Road,
Din Daeng, Bangkok 10400 Thailand
admin@teacarchitect.com, www.ap.tu.ac.th

VaSLab (1999)
3 Soi Punnavithi 12, Sukhumvit 101, Bang Chak,
Phra Khanong, Bangkok 10260 Thailand
vaslab@vaslabarchitecture.com, www.vaslabarchitecture.com

Vasu Virajsilp   Principal
Boonlert Deeyuen   Principal

Thonsilp Studio (1997)
199 Akarnsongkroh 14 Road, Thung Wat Don
Sathorn, Bangkok 10120 Thailand
thonsilp_s@yahoo.com

Chatree Ladalalitsakun

Photography Credit

Picture credits are listed by photographer alphabetically. All illustrations have been supplied courtesy of the architects. Photographic sources are listed where possible, but the publisher will endeavor to rectify any inadvertent omission.

Airports of Thailand
Suvarnabhumi International Airport

Architects 49
BU Landmark Complex
Central Plaza Khon Kaen
Energy Complex
King Power Complex
The 49 Terrace

B-1 Magazine
Baan Jew
The Office Plus

Baan Lae Suan
4C House

Beer Singnoi
Suvarnbhumi Honda Automobile
The 49 Terrace

Buchachon Petthanya
Ratchadalai Theater

Chana Sumpalung
Baan Bang Sarae
Baan Pracha Uthit

Chanathip Nantachaibancha
A Camouflage House

Chanok Thammarakkit
The Retreat

Ded Charoenlarp
Banyan Golf Clubhouse

Four Seasons
Cape Sienna Phuket Hotel

Jaratkul Juisiri
Plearnwan

Jaroonrat Vithoosuwan
Habormall
Prakit House

Jeravej Hongsakul
C House
Phuket Gateway

Kanate Chainapong
Arsom Silp Institute of the Arts and Development
Baan Huen Tham (The House of Dharma)
Community Organization Development Institute (CODI)
Samui International Airport
Yaiya Resort

Kasit Saengmukdah
Manarom Hospital
PM Center Office Building

Kiattipong Panchee
Six Senses Hideaway

Kiattisak Veteewootachan
Baan Pracha Uthit
The Emporio

Krissada Boonchaleaw
Baan Bang Sarae
Baan Pracha Uthit
Central Plaza Khon Kaen
Energy Complex
Suvarnabhumi International Airport
The Emporio

Martyn Goodacre
Baan Suriyan Chandra

Metric
Six Senses Hideaway

Narute Pongchavanakul
Banyan Golf Clubhouse
K Village

Oman Mirzaie
Cape Sienna Phuket Hotel

Pattarphon Sukjan
Crew Training Center (Renovation)

Pisan Khondee
The Emporio

Pongpon Yuttharat
Baan Sam Kanan (3 Parallels House)
Operation Center

Pruk Dejkhamhaeng
Plearnwan
U House

Rattapol Pattanarangsan
Satin Textile Worker Multi-Family Housing

Siam Paragon
Siam Paragon Shopping Center

Skyline Studio
PM Center Building

Sheraton Krabi Beach Resort
Sheraton Krabi Beach Resort

Spaceshift Studio
4C House
Baan Bang Sarae
Baan Suan Nonsee
Bracket House
BU Landmark Complex
Bunker House
Deviated House
Henry B Thompson Building
Honda Big Wing
Phuket Gateway
Practika Factory
Prakit House
Prince of Songkhla University International
Convention Center

Red Mountain Golf Club
Sala @ Sathorn
SCG Experience
Suvarnabhumi International Airport
Bangkok Panoramic view p.8-9

Sunan Prathakwanit
Manarom Hospital
PM Center Building

Surachai Akekapobyotin
Bangkok University Admission and
Information Center

Surachai Supasripipat
Sala @ Sathorn

Teerawat Winyarat
Royal Archive

Warawut Awutchanakarnkul
Cape Sienna Phuket Hotel

Wirachai Pranveerapaibool
Cape Sienna Phuket Hotel

Wison Tungthunya
Ayodhaya Links Clubhouse
Baan Windmill
Bangkok University International
College and Art Gallery
Bank of Thailand Headquarter
Banyan Golf Clubhouse
Esplanade & Ratchadalai Theatre
King Power Complex
Mini Showroom
Sala Phuket
Six Senses Hideaway
SUN ONE
The 49 Terrace

Worrawut Santikun
Chang House

Nithi Sthapitanonda
Editor

Presently 63 years old, Nithi received B.Arch from Chulalongkorn University's Faculty of Architecture, then, M.Arch. from the School of Architecture at University of Illinois in the US. At age 36, he established an architectural firm called Architects 49.

With professional organizations, Nithi was elected president of The Association of Siamese Architects under Royal Patronage (ASA) at age 45; became the secretary of Architect Council of Thailand at age 53; then, at age 55, was designated a National Artist in the field of Architecture (Contemporary).

In the realm of education, Nithi currently seats in Board of Trustees of Silpakorn University and Bangkok University. He, from 2006 to 2009, was the chairman of a judge committee for 'Designer of the Year Award' held by Silpakorn University. In 2010, he is also the chairman of a judge committee for the prestigious Silpathorn award, held by the Ministry of Culture.

Internationally, Nithi joined the Hon.FJIA (Honorary Fellow of The Japan Institute of Architects) in 1995 and the Hon.FAIA (Honorary Fellow of The American Institute of Architects) in 2008. In addition, The a+d & Spectrum Foundation of India bestowed on him in 2008 'the Golden Award for Excellence in Architecture 2007'.

In 2006, Nithi founded Li-Zenn Publishing Limited to produce architecture, art, history and culture books worldwide. He has produced and written more than 15 books, most of which are highly acclaimed locally and internationally, such as Architecture of Thailand (2005), Conversations with Architects (2007), Nithi Architectural Sketch Book (2007), Architectural Drawings of Historic Buildings and Places in Thailand (2008), Houses by Thai Architects (2008) and Resorts by Thai Architects (2009).

Editor
Nithi Sthapitanonda

Project Editor
Suluck Visavapattamawon

Associate Editor
Pisut Lertdumrikarn

Project Coordinator
Bussara Keamapirak

Editorial Team
Kloykamol Siribhakdi
Ruechimon Thanaboonsombut
Natcha Nantakarn

English Text edited by
Marcos Antonio Perez
Jon Sealey

Translation (Preface)
Kumari Ratanadib

Book & Layout Design
Yingyos Charubusapayon

Design Assistant
Vatanya Bongkotkarn

Drawing
Pongpanich Lerkpitukpanich
Acharawun Udomkham
Sansanee Bongkotkarn

Sponsor Coordinator
Jaruwan Punyoyai
Poonnabha Riantthong
Witsanee Kaewsomboon

Concept & Art Direction
Yingyos Charubusapayon

Li-Zenn Publishing Limited

Publisher
Nithi Sthapitanonda

Managing Director
Suluck Visavapattamawon

Deputy Managing Director
Pisut Lertdumrikarn